DATA EMBEDDING PROCESS OF RDH ALGORITHM

AF865797

BY

JEAN KATO

TABLE OF CONTENTS

Chapter - 1

INTRODUCTION

1.1 OVERVIEW OF DATA HIDING

In our society and lives the considerable changes is brought by the revolution based on digital content. Due to the many advantages of digital content, the data is generated from modern challenges and opportunities for research and innovation, because of the wide applications in steganography and watermarking in present days. The data is in the form of image, video and audio etc. In general data hiding schemes are changed cover content of image, video and audio etc. This is used for the purpose of embedding the data for security. The embedded data can be content owner identity, secret data and cover content information etc., based on the applications. The embedding scheme is designed for the broadly used applications of the data embedding schemes like medical imaging, fine arts, multimedia archive management, authentication, copyright protection, communication in military, remote sensing, broadcast monitoring, secret communication, finger printing and copy protection etc.[61,18].

The large amount of data is associated with the images, videos etc., when they are represented in digital form. For effective transmission and storage [3, 54] the compression standards usage is in demand such as JPEG, MPEG, JVT etc., In the recent unavoidable relationship of compression technique with multimedia data embedding became active area of research in the compressed domain. In both the domains of uncompressed and compressed the data can be embedded. In compressed domain as per its compression technique, the embedding data depends on its own merits and demerits [49].

The JVT, H.261, ITU, MPEG, JPEG, and H.263 etc. are all these compression standards are used in frequency domain to transfer the data. The DCT (Discrete Cosine Transform) is widely used standard transforms the pixels from spatial to frequency domain, the transform coefficients are quantized followed by encoding operation to compress the data. In quantized DCT coefficients, the data is embedded in a particular form and it is the most common practice which motivates for the purpose of achieving robustness. With the bit rate control and compression technique, the data embedding is associated especially in real time implementations. Embedding the data into digital content for steganography and watermarking is a challenging task because in data hiding schemes, the trade-off occurs in between embedding capacity and visual quality.

Both in compressed and uncompressed domain, an irreversible, reversible and near reversible manner are used to embed data. The original form of the data is not restored, when the data is embedded in irreversible form. But in some application like multimedia archive management, fine arts, military communications, medical imaging etc., after receiving the embedded data [34,35,36,29,74,39,73], the original content restoration is needed by the reversible data embedding schemes. For the applications such as remote sensing, biometric authentication etc. the permissible level of modification is accepted after the extraction. To recover the appropriate content [80,23,75] in this kind of applications, near reversible data hiding is employed.

Irreversible, reversible and near reversible data embedding schemes are given to a great extent in the state of frequency domain, because of wide usage of frequency transformation. In combination with digital data and in the perception of its requirements in aimed applications and along with robustness, on reversible data hiding in the frequency domain, data can be embedded in two trends in frequency domain. In first trend, spatial domain transform to frequency domain where the pixels values are transformed into the coefficients of the corresponding frequency domain and the data is embedded and in the second trend, the compression standard is utilized to transfer the data embedding into frequency domain. .

several requirements of both steganography and watermarking schemes, between the embedding capacity and visual quality there is a little difference. But entire focus is on the embedding capacity and visual quality.

The achievement of reversibility became a limiting factor for the visual quality because the additional modifications are involved in embedding the data. It means achieving higher embedding capacity becomes the first limitations to increase the visual quality in a similar way by achieving the reversibility, near reversibility a second limitation. This will enhance the visual quality. A balance is to be maintained in the middle of visual quality, embedding capacity and also the balance between visual quality and reversibility is highly important to consider. All the three requirements are influenced by the method of embedding and by utilizing the HVS characteristics. The utilization of underlying cover content for embedding the data, the visual quality is achieved.

There is an improvement in visual quality during the process of embedding the data by using a particular HVS characteristics. The evaluation parameter like visual quality metric is used to evaluate the distorted cover content because of embedding must also take into account, and the distortions effects in the corresponding HVS characteristics. In this thesis several data embedding schemes for digital content like image and video using DCT are introduced. The schemes aim towards achieving the near reversibility and reversibility to the maximum extent. In order to balance the drawbacks that exist among the requirements of embedding capacity, reversibility, near reversibility and visual quality. For this proposed different data embedding schemes by using non-zero DCT coefficients, to removal ambiguity, minimizing of coefficients and also considering HVS based visual quality evaluation metrics to compute the digital distorted content like image and video. The common goal of this thesis is towards achieving the near reversibility and reversibility of the data embedding schemes in the frequency domain using DCT.

1.2 SIGNIFICANCE OF DATA HIDING

Because of wide utilization of digital content, some of the major security concerns are copy rights violation, privacy of the content. The two alternative techniques are used so that the security problems like the data hiding and cryptography are solved. For textual content security, the cryptography need to be robust and it has the following limitations:

- The techniques of cryptography are unbreakable, however by revealing the existence of the secret message [62, 85] the concentration of pirate is attracted due to the plainly visible encrypted text.
- The security mechanism i.e., in some countries [25,82] there is restriction on cryptography.
- The procure product in cryptography may be a pirate, the decryption key can be applied [61] so that we can obtain the unprotected copy of the content.
- In the process of cryptography, the data protection can be done effectively in the transmission in encrypted form, there is no more protection [61] for the content if it is decrypted.

The hiding of data is becoming popular day by day because of the cryptography limitations which are mentioned above. In data hiding technique some information is embedding into the digital content, like audio, video and images either perceptibly or imperceptibly. The figure 1.1(b) which describes the data hiding technique, by embedding data based on the attention of the perceiver which is not made by stego-object and this is the output of the data hiding process i.e., text, image in to cover content. [62, 85].

To Data hiding technique the Watermarking and Steganogrpahy are very strongly related and the great portion of overlap [61] is maintained by it. If the image is watermarked in watermarking then only the content of image can be extracted if at all there is a dispute [61, 85]. Where as in Steganography from figure 1.1(a), by the transmitter or sender is embedded to transfer the information secretly to receiver where one can extract the secret information.

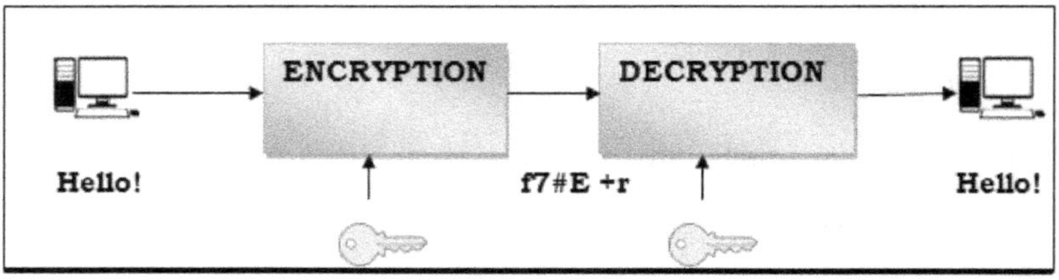

Fig 1.1: a) Encryption and Decryption of a message

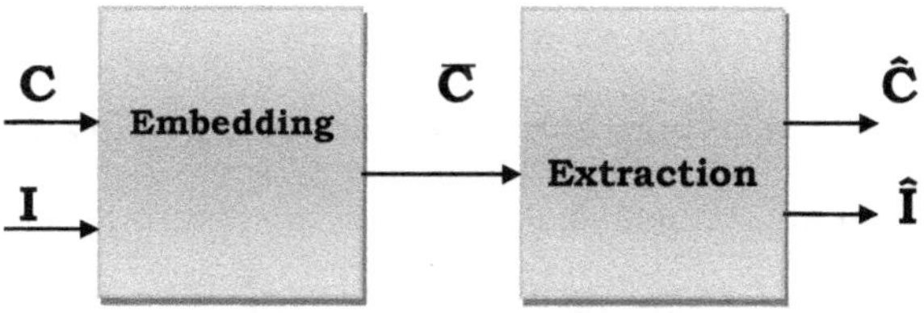

Fig 1.1: b) Generic Data Hiding Process

By using $(E(C,I) = C$ the general embedding procedure in data hiding techniques like watermarking and steganography is given and by using $D(C)= (\hat{C},\hat{I})$ the data can be extracted. where the Extracted data is given by $\hat{I}$ and after extracting the data $\hat{C}$ which is the cover object. In general, it can define the procedure of data extraction is reversible if $C=\hat{C}$ and $I=\hat{I}$, and if the values are relatively small then it is known as near reversible otherwise it is irreversible.

The data hiding significance includes steganography and watermarking and it is given as "In the recent past few years, digital images captured without difficulty with digital cameras, scanners, camcorders, and passed easily over the internet. As a result digital images appear in the internet and the WWW. With the large/maximum circulation of images, digital content may have security such as authentication, copy right violation and privacy" [40].

- The drawbacks of cryptography [62, 85] are addressed by data hiding techniques.
- Into the cover content C the message M can be embedded to get stego-object S by using the data hiding techniques, it can be different from C by HVS and the existence of M in 'S' [16,37,,61,75] cannot be sensed by the illicit user.
- Data hiding provides authentication to the broadcast media such files are image, audio and video [30].

Various applications of data hiding are military communications, remote sensing, multimedia archive, medical imaging, covert communications, fine-arts, image integrity production, tamper proofing, copy control and finger printing [61, 75, 80, 63, 44]. In spite of diverse applications and advantages, in data hiding schemes there exist definite challenges. In the cover content, the data is embedded. At the end of receiving, the data is recovered based on the correct cover content and this is very challenging task. In applications like medical imaging, military, law enforcement etc. The exact recovery of cover content is required, in this kind of applications, RDH is employed in order to recover of cover content and embedded data. The remote sensing, bio-metric authentication etc., these are the applications where permissible level of modification is considered after extraction and in this kind of applications NRDH is employed for approximate recovery of cover content [23,75,80].

The major problem while embedding the data is noise addition, then the quantized DCT block maintains the balance between visual quality, embedding capacity, blocking artifacts and ambiguity. These plays very important role for reversibility, near reversibility to embedded the data in cover content using data hiding techniques [61,80,44,63,75,40,16,37,38,73,74,50].

Because of the loss of information which is caused either from replaced or discarded information, data hiding is obtained because they are not reversible.

1.3 STATEMENT OF THE PROBLEM

A phenomenal growth in the use and transfer of multimedia data over internet by the netizens, not only increased the opportunity to the social media, advertisement etc., but also increased threat to the authentication, integrity and security of the multimedia contents.

1.4 MOTIVATION

The propagation of digital multimedia like image, video and audio and the emergence of digital networks are used for copyright enforcement schemes. The owners of multimedia need to protect them against illegal duplication, distribution and other unauthorized usage. In some applications, the issues are not completely solved by conventional encryption and copy protection mechanisms. For security, authentication, copyright protection and fingerprint etc., acts as hopeful data hiding method which is proposed in recent times. Here in this dissertation, the concentration is focussed on data hiding scheme in the form of Reversible and Near Reversible. A class of processes is represented by using data hiding and cover images which are used to embed data. The hidden data are usually a sequence of binary bits. Here the content of these data is embedded, therefore no requirements of additional storage. The hidden data are invisible to human being but can be recovered by a computer program.

1.5 OBJECTIVES

Identification of an Effective Data Hiding Schemes for digital content, and the objective of this research work follows:

1. Our design aims at minimizing the alterations to the cover content by achieving reversibility and provides results in the trade-off between the visual quality and embedded capacity.
2. To propose a Reversible scheme which focuses on ameliorating visual quality by minimizing the usage of nonzero quantized DCT coefficients during the embedding process.
3. To improve the visual quality in terms of PSNR, a Zig-Zag scan is used and a polynomial based function is proposed to a Near Reversible Scheme.
4. To achieve the overall digital media quality and removing the blocking artifacts, for a Near Reversible Scheme using a mathematical function.

1.6 SCOPE OF THE RESEARCH

Basically research & investigation is the main idea of this thesis which evaluates the potential of digital data hiding for authentication, copy right protection, temper assessment and secured communication of information.

The main intention is to supplement the overview of technology and to make new sight on effective design strategies, they are variety of schemes which are designed for copyright protection and secured communications and at the end improved embedded capacity and visual capacity that serves the purpose of safe and secured communications schemes and techniques are transform domain techniques like Discrete Cosine Transform and reversible and near reversible schemes are used. The thesis is organized in such a way to depict the outline of various approaches which are used for data hiding. The results and algorithm design of the investigation are summarized below under various chapter heading.

1.7 CONTRIBUTIONS

- In general, because of the modifications to the cover content in the process of achieving reversibility results in visual degradation of the content. This is the trade-off.
- It is noticed QCIF formatted videos that most of the AC Coefficients in DCT Quantized blocks are centered around the zero.
- The work balances the trade-off that exist between embedding capacity and visual quality.
- By considering above fact, we design a Reversible Data Hiding scheme (RDH) which uses the non-zero AC coefficient of quantized DCT blocks the same is presented in chapter 3.
- Achieving reversibility usually involves the modification of non-zero coefficients, during the elimination of ambiguity. This result in more visual distortions. To address above issue a reversible data embedding

scheme is proposed by minimizing the use of non-zero coefficients to ameliorate the visual quality the scheme is named as Ameliorate Visual Quality (RDH_AVQ) and it is presented in chapter 4.

- Near reversible data hiding scheme is another type of data hiding technique which further reduces modifications to the original content Thereby, improved the visual quality. The near reversible scheme is presented in chapter 5.
- Modification to the non-zero AC coefficients results in blocking artifacts. In order to remove the blocking artifacts and to achieve better visual quality. A mathematical function is proposed and it is presented in the chapter 6.

1.8 APPLICATIONS OF DATA HIDING

The broadcast monitoring, authentication, ownership protection, access/copy control, finger printing are the general applications of digital watermarking and assessment of Quality of Service (QoS) for particularly multimedia signal especially in mobile communication and radio environment. Few of the digital watermarking applications are elaborated much clear here:

Copyright Protection

The prominent application of watermarking is copyright protection, the ultimate objective is to embed the data. In order to resolve rightful ownership, the watermarks should survive against greater degree of signal distortions and even the watermarks must be in a position to establish rightful ownership under any circumstances. There are two broad categories of protection which measure via protection against piracy and protection in unauthorized usage. For this application, the main motivation is the web where the millions of freely available images are contained by the owner and they have to protest them.

Copy protection

The unauthorized copying of the media is allowed with the help of copy protection mechanism and is a desirable features distribution of multimedia system. it is not easy to achieve copy protection in open system where as it is feasible in closed or proprietary systems. This kind of watermarks indicates the copy status of the data, copy protection can occur at different stages, during the recording and playing back [13]. In this each case there is the presence of a potentially specific watermark, which can be used introduce a desired behaviour of operation controlling of devices.

Authentication

Due to recent improvement in digital technique have made, it much easier with digital works to get the interference in many ways. The aim of authentication is to detect the modifications [20, 14, 26, 27, 5]. Hash functions of cryptography and digital signatures provides both efficient and effective protection for applications the areas in which bitwise identity and authentication of digital document is required. In spite for the most of application which involves multimedia signals different types of modifications such as compression, provides in a bitwise difference between signals the generated signal and it is still considered to be authentic, and integrity is not violated. A possible solution may be to design a fragile watermark, in which authentications marks became failure as invalid. With the small modification of the cover content out of all possible watermarking applications. The low level of resiliency is required by this application. So, if a watermark is modified which contain the digital data, the watermark is modified along with it and makes the possibility of learning more about how the data is tampered.

Fingerprinting

Another promising application of digital watermarking is fingerprinting. Related to the legal recipient the information is conveyed. To trace back illegally produced copies of data carrying various watermarks used distributed copy based on application used. The main principles of such a watermarking algorithm are to have higher resilience against collusions attacks [28, 41]. Fingerprint watermarks can be embedded to a specific user at the distributions, which requires a considerable computational overhead in the process of generation of watermark and distribution media. This will permits the efficient creation of distinct copies on the other side and this kind of applications requires ease of extraction of the watermark with minimum complexity.

Secured Communication

Another interesting application of data hiding is to convey information to a group of friendly or single receivers. The term "steganography" instead of watermarking is more suitable for such applications of data hiding.

QoS Assessment

Due to unconventional use of digital watermarking in the recent past years for signals in mobile and multimedia applications the Quality of Services (QoS) became crucial. A reference watermark is available to the end user or mobile station which is embedded in the cover signal. With same channel degradations the watermark, in this alteration watermark denotes the states of the wireless. It is to mention that, this kind of watermarks should have low complexity, computations in the watermarking embedding and decoding.

Broadcast Monitoring

For the purpose of broadcast monitoring many organizations will come forward. The human observers are required by low technological method. This performs broadcast monitoring to watch and record the broadcast. This method is expensive for error prone and requires automated monitoring. The active monitoring system and passive monitoring system are the two types of techniques which are designed, along with the content associated information which is broadcasted. The active monitoring depends whereas in passive monitoring systems the content is being broadcasted directly recognized. Hence, watermarking is clear alternative method for information coding identification for active monitoring [15].

1.9 ORGANIZATION OF THESIS

The thesis entitled as "Identification of an Effective data hiding schemes for video" is divided into seven chapters. The brief report of all chapters is given in subsequent sections.

Chapter 1 In this Chapter data hiding concepts is explained briefly. Here, the frequency domain data hiding techniques provides various challenges. A brief review is given on the data hiding techniques which is classified based on Quantization and other techniques. Then next section focuses on contributions of the present work. Finally, this gives organization of thesis.

Chapter 2 presents the review of the existing Frequency domain quantization which is based on Data Hiding Techniques. The shortcomings of existing system are also explained.

Chapter 3 For MPEG-4 Video the work done on the RDH_NZAC data hiding technique is covered. In this chapter, illustrate on the embedded is given to DCT domain, to achieve reversibility the modification to be minimal. A better trade-off between visual quality and embedded capacity is resulted. Using RDH_NZAC embedding and extraction algorithms the proposed scheme provides visual quality, embedded capacity improvement. The subsequent sections present the RDH_NZAC technique results and with C.C. chen et.al., techniques these are compared.

Chapter 4 covers the proposed data hiding technique of RDH_AVQ. In this technique the use of non-zero coefficients is minimized. In the middle-frequency coefficients the data is embedded and thus all the process is done. When the ambiguity is eliminated where the terms of PSNR, SSIM, and SSIM_INDEX shows and improves the visual quality of digital media. By using RDH_AVQ technique, the embedding and extraction algorithm provides the reversibility and visual quality. The subsequent sections present the results of RDH_AVQ with S.gujjunoori et.al., technique is compared.

Chapter 5 Discuss about NRDH_POLY data hiding technique, which achieves higher visual quality a polynomial based function. Here, where by using the NRDH_POLY embedding and extraction algorithm process is performed. Minimized the coefficients in between the original non-zero and embedded coefficients. In Further sections present the results of NRDH_POLY technique is provided and compared with Sagar et.al., technique.

Chapter 6 focuses on NRDH_MATH data hiding technique which is a new category scheme concentrates on achieving the better visual quality and removing artifacts of mathematical function which is proposed. The visual quality of the degraded content is accessed by using visual quality metrics which are HVS based. The subsequent sections present the NRDH_MATH embedding and extraction algorithms, results of NRDH-MATH technique and at last these are compared with S. Gujjunoori et. al., technique.

Finally, chapter 7 the thesis conclusion and future-work are specified.

Chapter - 2

LITERATURE SURVEY

2.1 INTRODUCTION

Data hiding information is always used nearly in every aspect of our daily lives. It is in the form of secret communication or writing, which have existed since ages. The goal of hiding data has been traced to ancient Greece, China, and India. In the history of data hiding [61], interesting discussions can be found. Here few examples which are used by the Chinese rulers to communicate secretly in thin sheets of silk or paper the messages are written, and into small balls these are made by the messengers these balls are swallowed, on a shaved head a message is written and then hairs are grown. The invisible inks method is one of the effective method today as it was years ago. Data hiding can be done in audio, video, and image and in many other form of communication. Some data hiding techniques like Digital data hiding has potential for solving some important problems like content authentication, and digital rights management, and several emerging applications such as annotation of images and seamless upgrade of multimedia, have made sure that the interest in this field keeps growing. In the short survey presented here, we focus mainly on the techniques that are closely related to the data hiding presented in this thesis.

2.2 DATA HIDING KEY TERMS

Two common domains of operation are there in lossless embedding techniques are spatial and frequency. The spatial domain is used to embed the data on the individual pixel values and it directly operates, the embedded image (output image) and exhibits poor tolerance towards various external attacks such as compression, addition of noise, scaling, cropping, filtering and rotation. When the pixel values are multiplied in spatial domain, the content of the cover image may get affected. Hence in sensitive applications such as medical, military etc., embedding data in spatial domain may lead to misinterpretation of data. Here in frequency methods the performance of certain transforms and after modifications the message is embedded in the frequency coefficients of cover image. When compared with the spatial embedding schemes the transform embedding methods are more robust. In image-processing different types of attacks used in the spatial embedding schemes which are susceptible. In general higher capacity is provided by the spatial data hiding techniques, and it also defines the number of bits which can be embedded into the signal. For the quality measure known as perceptibility capacity, this is closely connected to the visually unacceptable level whether by embedding information provided by source cover which is distorted or not is shown by perceptibility or fidelity. The definitions and notions [39] of the below terms need to be summarized so that in data embedding one can get a brief idea about data hiding process:

- **Reversibility:** The image/Video is same as before embedding and after embedding is known as Reversibility.

- **Near Reversibility:** The digital media before embedding and after embedding is almost the same is known as Near Reversible.
- **Perceptibility:** Between the original, stego images, the resemblance is shown by Perceptual.
- **Payload:** Without including the redundant information the number of encoded bits of a watermark is defined.
- **Robustness:** After completion of operation of common signal processing the capacity of detecting the watermark is Robustness.
- **Capacity:** As the no. of bits which is to be embedded is defined as capacity.

By the complexity, visual quality and payload capacity limit, the data hiding methods performance may be studied [66], where after the completion of embedding operation, the stego image quality is shown by visual quality, and a number of mathematical operations is known as complexity.

2.3 FREQUENCY DOMAIN TECHNIQUES

In spatial domain, during the process of modifying the values of pixels there is a chance that original content may get affected. It lead to misinterpretation of embedding data in spatial domain of data in sensitive applications such as medical, military, etc. There are own advantages and disadvantages associated with each technique in the frequency domain. Modify the cover image by applying specific transformation function. They are designed against various geometrical transformations and external attacks they might be imperceptible and robust. For decomposition and reconstruction frequency domain based data hiding transform is used. The Discrete Cosine Transform (DCT) is a transform which is used when the frequency coefficients of the cover images and the secret data is to be embedded. To high frequency, mid band frequency and low frequency components the transformation of image can be decomposed. Depending on the application, the increased flexibility as choice of an ideal embedding location is provided by the decomposition or separation of frequencies. For different data hiding schemes, a common practice as followed to transform the specific application by choosing appropriate data hiding to obtain optimal embedding results due to the unique nature of DCT transform.

2.3.1 Classification of Frequency Domain Data Hiding

In the last few decades [61,80,44,47,59,52], the enormous significance is gained by the art of secretly hiding and communicating data. Due to its fast access capability, the communication of digital information become frequent in now-a-days. In modern communication, the resistance of data protection is necessary. As Irreversible, Reversible and Near Reversible, the classification of data hiding schemes can be in frequency domain. The hiding scheme can be judged generally using the visual quality metrics.

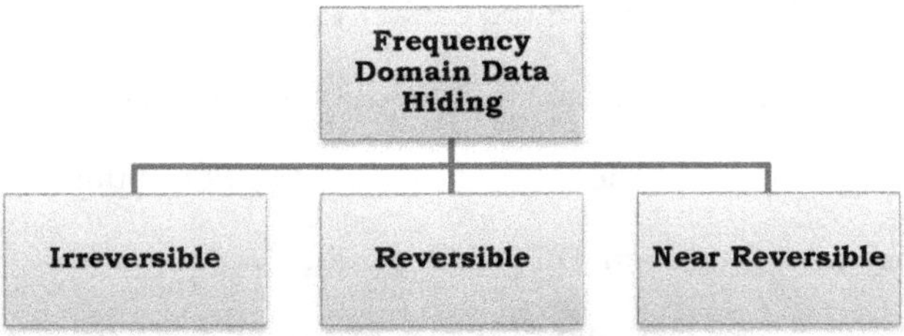

Fig: 2.1: Classification of Frequency Domain Data Hiding

Irreversible: The restored and original cover content completely differ after extraction.

Reversible: The scheme which restores the cover content after the extraction.

Near Reversible: after extraction the scheme in which the restored cover content is nearer to the original cover content.

2.3.2 DCT Based Schemes

Cox et. al., [7] used frequency domain techniques for exploiting the possible locations to embed secret bits. To the payload by embedding a pseudo random sequence corresponding mid band coefficients, the DCT transformed host image is used by the Barni et. al., [12]. The resultant embedded image offered robustness towards aggressive operations of image processing like scaling, compression, cropping, rotation, etc., Fridrich et. al., [29] the scheme of watermarking is presented on the basis of Discrete Cosine Transform [DCT). In the domain of JPEG, the digital images are authenticated. The quantization table is modified by using this scheme and per chosen by DCT coefficient where the lossless embedding of one bit is enabled. By dividing the cover image into blocks which is introduced by this

Chang et. al., [56] will increase the capacity of data embedding. Xuan et. al., [58] have used a histogram pair to hide data and by selecting threshold and JPEG coefficient region. The data is applied to JPEG quantized 8 x 8 block DCT coefficients. Based on DCT. Lin et. al., [70] there is a proposal of a technique called reversible data hiding in which an image block will provide one secret bit which was embedded into two neighbouring DCT coefficients. A high degree of robustness is exhibited towards a wide range of aggressive image processing operations.

2.4 REVERSIBLE DATA HIDING

After extraction process the recovering of original image called Reversible data hiding such as multimedia archive management, remote sensing, medical imaging, military etc., these are RDH data hiding techniques [36,74,73,77,79,19]. In general, with limited embedding capacity, the more modifications of cover content was lead by the reversibility. However, the reversibility is needed to some applications to work on large data.

The earliest reference to digital content authentication with data hiding could find is Barton patent field in 1997 [8]. Then, to address lose of information which is caused by data embedding. To recover the original image content in lossless manner, the path is driven by reversible data hiding by C.W.Honsinger et. al.,., [32]. Without compression by C. De Vleeschouwer et. al.,., [43] a data hiding technique is proposed. In this technique, the cover content watermark payload or a binary pattern is embedded. Here, the small amount of data is hidden in which with a block in the cover content consists of the each bit which is associated and restricted for chosen set of images. Here, lossless content may be recovered. With many new inventions and improvements and with existing techniques or extending existing techniques, RDH techniques have been developed. Based on past reviews of RDH [80, 53, 71, 67].

Rebecca Dhupppe et.al.,[84] Introduced reversibility to achieve embedding data in reversible data embedding scheme which causes distortions in digital media. The distortions are due to occurrences of repetitive geometric patterns. For an embedding scheme, there is a need of reversible enhancement schemes so that it may reveal the existence of hidden data and the visual quality which is neglected and other features which consider during embedding. The scheme of reversible enhancement is desirable for application like satellite, medical etc. To improve the capacity this is the first work which is useful so that a good visual quality is maintained.

Sagar G et.al.[81] they proposed two embedding schemes referred to MIDCAP and MIDVIS. During MPEG-4 compression the coefficients of quantized DCT having middle frequency which is used by these schemes to embed the data. To improve embedded capacity MIDCAP is used and to improve the visual quality MIDVIS is used. They embedded the data only into non-smoother blocks achieved by the embedded capacity but which requires better visual quality. Proposed schemes are achieved by reversibility processs.

S. Gujjunoori et.al.,[76] When the raw YUV video is compressed into MPEG-4 format, then the data is embedded into MPEG-4 video. Followed by encoding the intra coded and inter coded frames which is contained by the Framework of MPEG-4. The prediction, DCT, embedding, quantization, and encoding are included in it. Using the DCT in frequency domain, the data is embedded then the visual quality of the content can't be alone done by PSNR. Exactly in the middle sets the proposed scheme uses the multiple bits which are embedded. This results shows the visual quality. The PSNR is measured by widely used visual quality and for the purpose of evaluating the distorted image/video content quality it is not suitable. The other metrics HVS are used to access overall evaluation of multimedia content. In terms of metrics of HVS, the higher embedded capacity and obtained one can achieve the good visual quality. Another measurement is used for evaluating the performance of data embedding scheme.

Hui C et.al.,[64] These to MPEG-4 format uses the YUV format to compress the video. Two watermarks are used to authenticate the video. The quality of subsequent frames is degraded because of distortions in the frames due to data hiding.

C. C. Chen and D.S Kao [55] They proposed three rules. The ZRE, ZRX are the two rules used to embed and extract one bit coefficients and during embedding and extraction the confusion is prevented by CA rule. On quantized DCT coefficients, the proposed reversible image watermarking approach works. One bit is embedding into three sequences numbers of the quantized DCT coefficients. When embedded bits are increased then there is a decrement in PSNR value. The quality of the watermark is acceptable and regions of malicious attack are detected.

Nikolay P et.al.,[60] Based on a HVS the coefficient of contrast masking of DCT basis functions acts as simple and effective model. In comparison to known metrics there is higher efficiency for new measure PSNR-HVS-M. The new metric could be convenient and understandable.

J Feng et.al.,[53] based on past reviews of RDH. RDH classified into 4 categories and those are Data embedding at edges, Difference Expansion, quantization based data hiding techniques and histogram modification.

H-W. Tseng et. al.,[48] A method of data hiding having high capacity is proposed by this method and the JPEG compressed image will provide the secret data which is embedded. The embedded capacity is quite limited because in quantized DCT components the fixed size of secret data is embedded by traditional schemes. For each DCT component adaptive capacity estimation is conducted to improve the embedded capacity and the balance between image quality and embedding capacity is maintained by adjusting capacity factor. With little noticeable degradation of image quality, the compression ratio is low and High Embedded capacity around 20% of JPEG Compressed image size the scheme is achieved.

2.5 NEAR-REVERSIBLE DATA HIDING

Here, certain level of modification is defined by the application. These data hiding techniques are called near-lossless or semi-reversible or Near Reversible Data Hiding (NRDH) technique, not necessary to accomplish the reversibility requirement. Due to limitations involved in the Reversible Data Hiding (RDH), NRDH category techniques are gaining importance. Changing of original content into some extend is acceptable. It has emerging application in remote sensing images [7].

S.Gujjunoori and B.B. Amberker [75] have proposed a simple near reversible data embedding scheme which embeds the data during the process of MPEG-4 compression of digital video. They used non-zero AC elements of quantized DCT coefficients in the middle frequency region of DCT blocks. Proposed design is reduced the modifications of all non-zero AC coefficients of original coefficients in the selected sets. They have taken QCIF formatted videos and compressed using standard MPEG-4 encoder. Their proposed method not only out performs in terms of embedded capacity by maintain the visual quality, Less complex scheme which is proposed almost reversible.

Zhang et. al.,. [69] Based on LSB replacement there is a proposal for near reversible watermarking algorithm. The watermarked image can well hide the information of watermark information and to a high extent the original host image can be restored and it is proven by simulation results. The watermarked image can well hide the data in same bit when the secondary LSB data of host image, watermark data are stored. In robustness and computational complexity of the algorithm can make a job to a high extent. Using this algorithm the original host image can be recovered and it is proven by simulation results and in computing complexity, hiding ability and robustness it had good performance. For this algorithm, the embedding capacity is decided by the ratio between the host image size and watermark.

Tang and Huang [57] assumed that the embedded image is not altered and such a constraint is sometimes considered unnecessary because as long as the image can be restored to an acceptable level, moderate alteration on the embedded image should be allowed. Such a reasoning leads to a new category of techniques called near-reversible data embedding, in which the embedded image is allowed to be manipulated and the image can be restored to some extent that is very close to the original image. In this paper, a near-reversible data embedding scheme is proposed based on projection histogram manipulations. Because the projection histograms are relatively stable under common image operations, the attacked image can be restored to a level which is very close to the original image. The capacity of the method depends on the number of available image blocks because only one bit is embedded into one block. The experimental results indicate that the proposed algorithm is very robust against blurring, sharpening, JEPG compression, noise addition, and adjustment of brightness and contrast. Furthermore, the embedded payload can be robustly extracted. Thus, investigation conducted is balanced among the embedding capacity, the image quality after restoration, and robustness.

Ahmed and Moskowitz [51] For the purpose of authenticating medical images a technique is proposed which is known as semi-reversible frequency domain digital watermarking. This approach is for protecting medical images in digital watermarking. Depending on applications there are different types of watermarking. Authentication watermark is used in the proposed work. Basically on frequency domain watermarking technique called phase mark is used. To original or cover media the watermark or signature is embedded by the embedded and the presence of watermark is detected by detector. The unfortunate side-effect is the degradation of cover image where the information is embedded. Some of the degradations have been fixed is major advantage of this method and by 3dB, the PSNR (a standard image quality metric) is improved. For the purpose of authentication of medical images the result is significant, where due to information hiding or watermarking the diagnostically unacceptable degradation is not tolerable.

Z Wang et.al.,[17] Due to the proposed SSIM indexing, the structural similarity implementation is completed. The concepts of Creative investigation of structural information and structural distortion are likely to be implemented.

Barni et. al.,. [37] have introduced the near-lossless paradigm for the first time. They noticed that the use of digital watermarking in the remote sensing field has been so far limited. In fact, in the past the scientific nature of remote sensing data has often been put forward as a reason to not modify these data in any way; more recently it has been recognized that, since these data are affected by inherent measurement noise, slight modifications can be accepted provided that suitable quality requirements are met. This led to the development of the so-called near-lossless concept, meaning that data modifications can be accepted, provided that at every pixel they are within a maximum user-defined distance from the original image. If this bound if sufficiently low, it is expected that the results of applications run on near-lossless processed images are extremely close to those related to the original unmodified data. In this paper they have extend the near-lossless concept to the digital watermarking scenario. In particular, they first rephrase the near-lossless concept in the watermarking field. Then, they proposed a modification of two well-established techniques originally developed to protect multimedia data. More specifically, near-lossless watermarking is achieved by clipping the watermark signal in the spatial domain so that the maximum signal distortion is kept below a user-specified limit. The impact of the clipping operation on watermark robustness is evaluated experimentally, as well as the impact of watermark insertion on a classical remote sensing application such as unsupervised classification. They showed that, by forcing a maximum absolute difference between the original and watermarked scene, the near-lossless paradigm makes it possible to decrease the effect of watermarking on remote sensing applications to be carried out on the images.

2.6 IRREVERSIBLE DATA HIDING

Some of the literature data hiding techniques are not so precise to restore the cover content C and message M after the extraction [77]. For some applications there might be restoration of cover content is not vital then the visual quality, embedding capacity, robustness, etc. these data hiding techniques are called Irreversible Data Hiding (IDH) techniques [66].

G K. Wallace [1] by this article one can get the overview of JPEG standard and on the simply lossy technique known as baseline method the focus is concentrated.

F A.P. petitcolas et.al.,[21] Here the overview of information hiding is general and steganography. A range of tools are provided by both historical precedent and recent innovations, which sufficiently to solve most the problems where we met in information hiding.

M. Barni et.al.,[33] In this paper for the remote sensing images the applicability of watermarking techniques are analyzed. ECMS based watermarking techniques proposed and the results of the applicative tasks are effected by the presence of watermark. Further to develop the watermarking techniques for remote sensing applications, optimum decoder structure is derived depending on statistical decision theory to obtained results. On a solid theoretical background, the time is develop to watermarking. The recovery of watermark standardization is needed in real world applications for the more effective use of watermarking technology.

J Fridrich et.al.,[35] On the basis of manipulation of quantization table for image authentication two invertible watermarking techniques are proposed. In some cases the proposed two techniques are invertible i.e., by removing authentication data with a very small and invertible distortion if the image is authentic the original image content can be restored.

J Tain [39] introduces large embedding capacity based on RDH technique using Difference Expansion. For the purpose of embedding the DE based techniques discovers extra storage area and concluded that when compared to previous data hiding techniques the embedding capacity, visual quality are among the best in this technique.

A Khan et.al.,[65] For decoding purpose the exploitation of ML concepts are there. To develop the watermarking system the SVM and ANN are used which are ML based techniques. In remote diagnosis aid and tele surgery applications, the image watermarking is implemented. But on a patient's life the message recovery performance will be the severe effect.

V Sachnev et.al.,[68] PE based data embedding processes consists of following steps i.e., identifying expandable locations, compress expandable pixels position values called Location Map(LM) and embed secret data and compressed LM into expandable locations. Then extraction process consists extract secret data from stego-object, then regenerate cover content.

C-C Lin et.al.,[72] A notation based data hiding scheme is proposed by dividing the coefficients in the six sub areas in the DCT based image. But for data hiding there is usage of only five sub areas.

F Huang et.al.,[83] currently the JPEG is the most popular used format. The compressed image more distortions may be introduced because of modifications in JPEG image. Instead of this Quantized DCT coefficients are considered. The less distortion is introduced by some zero coefficients may selected that may slightly increase file size.

2.7 SUMMARY

In this chapter, a brief overview of the frequency domain data hiding schemes and techniques that are closely related to the frequency domain data hiding schemes are proposed in this thesis. There are many issues that have not been addressed adequately in the state of the art. For example, an important point is to investigate the performance of practical image hiding schemes in the context of the capacities predicted by the information-theoretic analysis. We propose efficient data hiding schemes in the next chapter, which employs image/video adaptive criteria for embedding schemes.

Chapter - 3

REVERSIBLE DATA EMBEDDING SCHEME FOR MPEG-4 VIDEO USING NON-ZERO AC COEFFICIENTS OF DCT (RDH_NZAC)

3.1 INTRODUCTION

Digitizing video: Definitions and Quality considerations

Digital video is an illusion. Digital video [86] is a filmstrip and the screen of each frame is projected at the rate of 24 frames per second. The same operation is performed by television and it projects 30 frames per second. To digitize each image/frame, the basic concept in digitizing motion video and at a quick enough rate is shown to the viewer. Basically, for smooth motion at least 12 to 15 frames are needed per second.

To reduce the data, compression helps but it is not enough. To digitizing the video requires decisions to make how data to be reduced. The data rate can be determined by three factors:

• **The size of the video window**. Usually 320 x 240 pixels is largest window size. There is a need of lower date rate for small window.

• **The frame rate of the digital movie** At 10 fps or 15 fps the majority of movies are displayed.

• **The picture quality** indicates that what the compression is used.

The aim of the data rate is to determine how the movie is delivered and stored. Image and video compression appear to survive with this data rate because of the lossy compression techniques. With the use of signal transforms one can utilize Human Vision (HV) properties for every image or video frame it is the fundamental idea, so that in space and time the input is represented in a hierarchical or layered representation and in a small percentage of transform coefficients the major part of visual information will be clustered and in a sparse representation the remaining coefficients are there. With selection of techniques the representation of transforms are effectively quantized and coded. Moreover, an amount of the transform-coefficient information is unnoticed depend on the available bandwidth. On the performance of the utilized motion estimation model, the transform coding techniques the performance of input video is visually near lossless representation and finally after decoding the input video can be obtained. When compensation techniques and motion estimation are used the sparseness is significantly increased. Here in case of video view, the temporal similarities are exploited among neighbouring frames based on transform domain representation.

3.2 ESSENTIAL REQUIREMENTS FOR VIDEO [86]

The four spatial resolution levels should support for scalable video coding technology [86] which could range from 1152×1408 to 144×176 pixels. The QCIF and CIF used formats which are commonly used at the low-end of the scalability system. In a variety of applications, the multiple resolutions from one bit stream are important. For example, distribution and multi-channel content production used for different video resolutions, from Personal Digital Assistant (PDA) resolution to studio-profile down. In this manner, a single scalable bit stream used by different clients. Another essential application of resolution scalability is in the area of industrial monitoring systems and video surveillance is the usage of this functionality is two-fold.

- In a usual scenario, based on spatial scalability, multiple views from various locations are received at each monitoring station and each view can be enlarged on-the-fly, if it is essential. It is restricted the overall communication bandwidth between the monitoring stations and camera network, because higher-resolution content is transmitted based on request from the user or an alarm.

- Support for video storage space with disintegration functionality. The significance of the recorded data, and the required resolution of the recorded video sequences decreases over time in industrial monitoring systems and surveillance. For instance, for three days a full resolution video is stored, and older than that sequences are only required in a medium resolution. A minimal resolution may be required only for a medium-to-long-term archiving if the sequences are older than one week.

Requirements for Bitrate (Quality) Scalability

To occur in a fine-granular set of bitrates scalable coding permits the video transmission by representation of video into multiple qualities. MPEG requirements possess, a variety of bitrates provides by practical quality scalable coding schemes, which communicate to transmit rates afford by a variety of today's networks. It should be state that for certain video compression applications, such as the military surveillance, medical applications, and Digital Cinema industry or space exploration for lossless coding should be supported. Over unreliable networks and content distribution, the broad area of video transmission is involved by the main applications of quality scalability. When on-the-fly adapting the quality of the transmitted video large bandwidth fluctuations can be effectively handled and more bandwidth and storage is required to charge a different fee for higher quality content requiring. For different quality levels one bit stream should be provided.

Requirements for Frame-rate (Temporal) Scalability

Replay frame-rate and regulate the transmission consists of a capable way for changing the video quality perceived by human observers. In adding up, the same video sequence for different frame-rates corresponds to different complexity profiles for decoding. As a result, it is recognized that scalable video coding should support at least four levels of temporal scalability, which can differ the decoding frame-rate dynamically. Moreover, with frame rates up to 60 Hz the decoding of moving pictures is done should be supported in order to satisfy a broad variety of video applications.

The multi-channel content production and distribution is the main application domains of demanding temporal scalability, where the different temporal resolutions use the same bit stream which will be viewed for a variety of supporting devices. Lastly, temporal scalability is very useful where cameras are usually monitoring static areas and high frame-rate video is required only after an alarm is activated. The application areas that involve resolution scalability, such as surveillance and monitoring applications.

3.3 YUV VIDEO FORMAT [64,76]

As part of a color image pipeline YUV is used and it is a color encoding system. The certain YUV standards are confirmed by photographic equipment or interfacing with digital television behind implementing or investigating properties of YUV.

In computer industry the commonly used term is YUV where using YCbCr the file-formats are encoded. For the purpose of color information digital encoding the YCbCr is used and for video and still-image compression it is suited, in PAL composite color video (excluding PAL-N) standard the utilization of YUV color model is done. In terms of two chrominance (UV) and one luminance (Y) components the color space is defined by YUV. The utilization of one luminance (Y) information is in systems of previous black-and-white. When through a sub-carrier the color information (U and V) was added separately.

In a YUV format Digital video is often encoded. With the utilization of primary color values an RGB color is encoded. For visible spectrum portions these values correspond directly. A RGB color space shown in figure 3.1 is nothing but a mathematical coordinate system which is formed by the three RGB values. Here in the below coordinate system by red component one of the axis is defined, the second co-ordinate is defined by blue, and the third co-ordinate is defined by green. Within this color space any valid RGB color may fall.

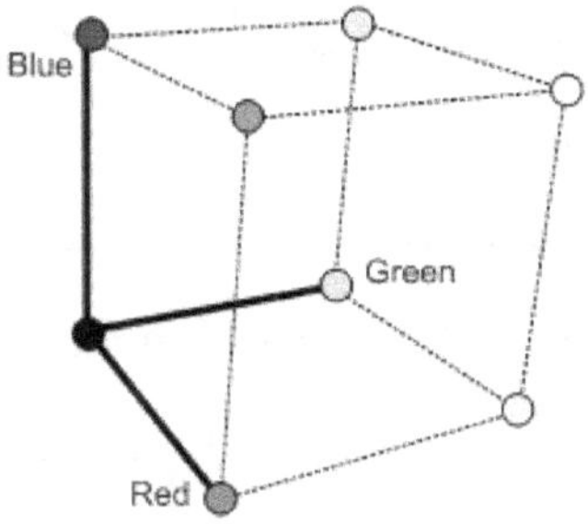

Fig: 3.1: RGB Color space

In most way the colors are represented by RGB format. A family of color spaces are referred by YUV, and from color information the brightness information is encoded separately. To represent any color YUV uses three values like RGB. As Y', U, and V these values are termed. (There is technical inaccuracy in the use YUV. The $Y'C_bC_r$ is one particular color space in computer video, the term YUV is referred as $Y'C_bC_r$.)

From linear RGB values luminance is derived. For true brightness the closer brightness is luminance but for technical reasons luma is more practical. There is a frequent imitation of prime symbol, but luma is always used by YUV color spaces but not luminance.

By taking the primary color (RGB) components weighted average the luma is derived from an RGB color.

3.3.1 How YUV Works?

The separation of luminance and chrominance characteristics is the most important difference between RGB and YUV, commonly referred to as luminance and chrominance in the analog (ie linear scaled) domain. The names luma and chroma are actually given for digital video to denote the use of Y', Cb, and Cr calculations vs. Y, Pb, and Pr. Since in green light waves most luma is actually perceived, and conversely most information the human eye perceives from the color green is luminance, from the chroma information completely green can be omitted. That leaves us with chroma components of only Red and Blue. As a channel each of the three components may also be referred, as in the Y (Luma) Channel, U (Blue) Channel, and V (Red) Channel.

The RGB can be converted to YUV and vice-versa using the following formulas:

From RGB to YUV

$Y = 0.299R + 0.587G + 0.114B$

$U = 0.492 (B-Y)$

$V = 0.877 (R-Y)$

It can also be represented as:

$Y = 0.299R + 0.587G + 0.114B$

$U = -0.147R - 0.289G + 0.436B$

$V = 0.615R - 0.515G - 0.100B$

From YUV to RGB

$R = Y + 1.140V$

$G = Y - 0.395U - 0.581V$

$B = Y + 2.032U$

3.3.2 Benefits of YUV

For historical reasons YUV is partly used by analog television. The television signals of anolog television are designed with black-and-white televisions they are backward compatible. Onto the signal of luma, the information of chroma (U and V) is superimposed and by the color television signal it is carried out. The chroma is ignored by black-and-white televisions and as a gray scale image the combined signal is displayed. The chroma can be extracted by Color televisions and back to RGB the signal is converted.

There is other advantage of YUV which makes it more relevant today. The changes in brightness to changes in hue will produce the human eye as less sensitive. As a result, without sacrificing the image perceived quality the luma can have more information than chroma. When compare with an RGB pixel a YUV pixel is of same size unless or until the chroma is down sampled. The RGB and YUV is not permanently packed. One of lossless conversion is the conversion from RGB to YUV. When compared with RGB and YUV pixel can be converted back with zero information loss if there is no down sampling. YUV image is made smaller by down sampling and color information is lost. However, the loss is not perceptually significant if down sampling performed correctly.

3.3.3 YUV Formats [64, 76]

- YUV 4:4:4
- YUV 4:2:2
- YUV 4:2:0
- YUV 4:1:1

Per pixel 24 bits are transmitted by the YUV444 data format. For each value of Y, U and V 1 byte is assigned, which makes it straightforward format to understand.

In the following manner the bytes are ordered in the image, where a single byte of color or brightness value is represented by Y, U, V, and 0, 1, 2... represent the pixel numbers associated with those values:

U0 Y0 V0 U1 Y1 V1 U2 Y2 V2...

Between two pixels the both U and V values are shared by the YUV422 data format. As a result, to the PC image these values are transmitted and once for every two pixels it buffers per pixel and produce average transmission rate of 16 bits.

In the following manner the bytes are ordered in an image:

U0 Y0 V0 Y1 U2 Y2 V2 Y3 U4 Y4 V4...

The chroma samples across both horizontally adjacent and vertically adjacent pixels are shared by YUV with a chroma sub sampling of 4:2:0. Only a single U/V chroma sample is contained by each 2x2 block of pixels.

3.4 INTRODUCTION TO MPEG [86]

The abbreviation of MPEG is Moving Picture Experts Group. The streams which are known as discrete data containers here the MPEG video and audio data are packaged. By playback applications it is made easy to switch between streams on the fly when video and audio streams are kept discrete. The two basic kinds of streams are supported by the MPEG formats and there are variations in each standard of MPEG.

Elementary streams: The video and audio elementary streams are combined or multiplexed together with the help of these streams. They are also known as applications must be able to demultiplex the streams back into the same. Only the elementary streams are played by some of applications.

3.4.1 MPEG-4 [79]

In MPEG-1 and MPEG-2 many of the features are inherited by the MPEG-4 and rich metadata, digital rights management (DRM), scene description, discrete object encoding these all are rich set of multimedia features which are added to MPEG-4. At low bit rates when compared to MPEG-1 and MPEG-2, the MPEG-4 video is compressed and the superior quality is provided. Only subsets of all the features which are available in MPEG-4 are supported by most of applications. However, high-resolution video is supported by MPEG-4. However, Motion JPEG is a large amount of image data and across the network. There is a advantage for MPEG standards when compared to motion MPEG and the advantages commences while a lower volume of data is sent per unit across the network and the advantage is exceptional at low frame rates. Between neighbouring frames to a high degree at low frame rates there are similarities and these are not utilized by the MPEG compression, and the consumption of bandwidth of MPEG is as same as motion MPEG because of the generation of overhead by the MPEG streaming format. In most cases than Motion JPEG the MPEG–1 is more effective However, the better image quality and advantages are provided by MPEG – which comprises of frame rate and resolution. The more network bandwidth consumption is required by MPEG-2 and the technique involved with complexity. A compression technique is offered called as the MPEG–4 which is developed. A like MPEG–1 and MPEG–2 it delivers the video compression. The MPEG may act as the preferred option under the following conditions if at a high frame rate the video need to be recorded or if there are storage space restraints or if there is a limitation for bandwidth of available network. At a lower bit-rate (bandwidth usage) a relatively high image quality is provided by it. Still, in encoding and decoding there is a demand for lower bandwidth's but it involves higher complexity, and when compared to JPEG it contributes to a higher latency.

3.5 C.C CHEN SCHEME

In general, to the cover content more modifications are caused when the reversibility is achieved and it results in visual degradation. Between the visual quality & embedding capacity the trade-off is occurred. Therefore, for MPEG-4 video the designing ways need to be explored to design a reversible data embedding scheme so that the trade-off is maintained and here in this process into quantized DCT coefficients when the data is embedded. In a quantized DCT block most of the AC coefficients are centered on zero and it is identified when most of the standard QCIF formatted videos are observed. A scheme of reversible data embedding is designed by this observation and in the quantized DCT blocks where the non-zero coefficients are used by this scheme. While achieving the reversibility, the alterations to the cover be minimized this is the design's aim. The visual quality & embedding capacity are improved by the proposed scheme and it is compared with C-C Chen scheme [55].

3.6 RDH_NZAC SCHEME

When into MPEG-4 the raw YUV video is compressed during this compression process and MPEG-4 video data is embedded. In our proposed work the framework and models of sagar g et.al. Followed by encoding the frames formation of intra coded and inter coded are included in MPEG-4 by the embedding framework. Specially, the components like prediction, embedding, quantization, DCT, encoding are included in figure 3.2 these components are shown.

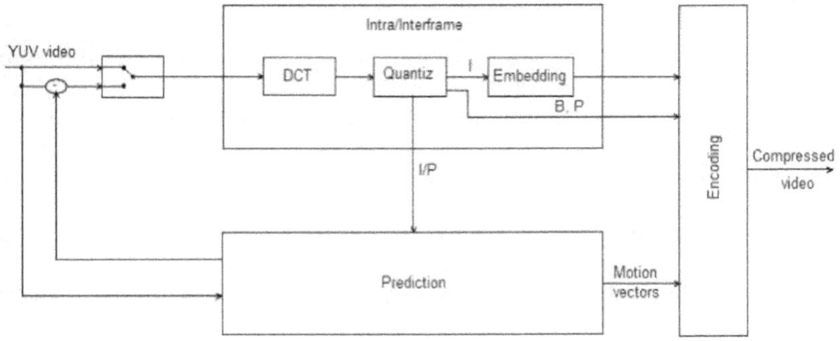

Fig: 3.2: The framework of embedding in MPEG-4

The sequence of frames is contained by the raw YUV video. Let for raw YUV video the sequence of original frames be like this $F=\{f_1,f_2,......f_n\}$, here the frames total number is given by n. The one luminance and two chroma components are contained by each frame fi $\in$ F. Let fi={Y,Cb,Cr}, where the luminance component is denoted by Y and two chroma components of fi are Cb,Cr. With the help of MPEG-4 encoder all these components are conveyed. To the MPEG-4 encoder as an input all the frames of F are given. As the sequence of I – P – B – frames and the frames in F are expressed by using encoder of MPEG-4 when the process of compression process is taking place. Then F=I U P U B where the reference frames is given by I and as the sets of P-B- frames the P,B act. For embedding we use only I frames and all the frames in F can also used. Let I= $\{I_1, I_2 \ldots I_m\}$, where $m<n$. As we concern with I, let $I_i=\{Y_i, C_{Ib}, C_{ir}\}$, where the luminance component of Ii is Yi and the two chroma components of Ii are C_{ib}, C_{ir}. For embedding the data the Y_i is considered. Here n_1 x n_2 is the size of Y_i and into 8 x 8 blocks of intensity values the size is partitioned. We assume that both n_1, n_2 are the multiples of 8. Here in the set I the blocks total number is given by m =m x l. As 2-dimensional DCT there is a transformation of 8 x 8 non- overlapping blocks. Here, in the special domain at the coordinate (x,y) for block B_{ij} the intensity values are given by $0 \leq u,v \leq 7$, and $B_{ij}(x,y)$ and at the coordinate (u,v) in the frequency domain $F_{u,v}$ represents the co-efficient. From low frequency to high frequency for 8 x 8 blocks is shown in Figure 3.3 [34,46]. Let the set of quantized DCT coefficients be D_k ($1 \leq k \leq 9$). For embedding the data these sets are used. Let in the set D_k the quantized DCT coefficient's sequence be $(d_{-k1}, d_{k2}, \ldots, d_{k,k(k)})$, where in Table 3.1 the $K_{(k)}$ is given. Let the data to be embedded be present in 𝕀.

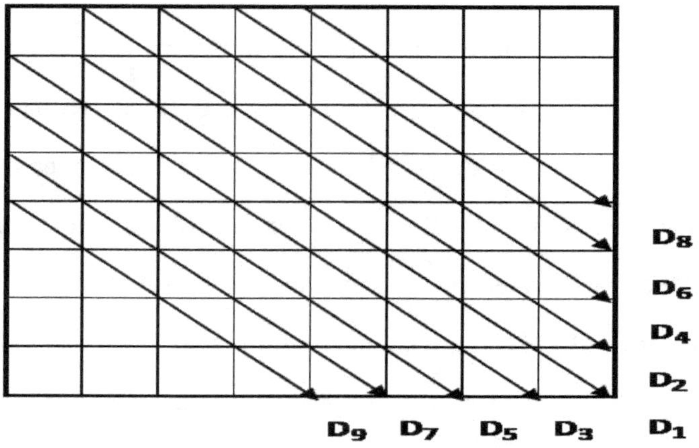

Fig: 3.3: chosen sets for embedding

Table 3.1: The size of the chosen sets for embedding

K	1	2	3	4	5	6	7	8	9
K(k)	7	7	7	6	6	5	5	4	4

3.6.1 Intra-frame Compression

Within the individual frames of video the encoding of data is the basis function for JPEG and MPEG and after the Discrete Cosine Transform [DCT] application followed by entropy encoding into similar patterns or sequences of pixels the individual blocks of image are shaped in mathematical short-hand these areas are described. A large amount of data is saved by this intra-frame compression [79]. To smooth the edges of macro blocks MPEG-4 includes an additional post-filtering stage and at higher compression ratios these are typically visible. The more advanced technique of intra-frame compression technique is wavelet which is included in JPEG-2000 and when compared to DCT compression it minimises blocky artefacts.

3.6.2 Inter-frame Compression

A hybrid encoding regime is supported by MPEG video compression, where not only the compression of individual frames is done, but also with similarities [usually within a shot or scene] the entire sequences of frames may be encoded. Under certain conditions that are at lower bit-rates these differences known as temporal or inter-frame [79] encoding techniques. For a given picture quality it requires less data, to encode every frame. Within macro blocks the groups of pixels are mapped by Inter-frame encoding and from one frame to the next [i.e. fixed backgrounds] it stays the same or which move in the same direction. Using motion vectors we can track their relative position rather than recoding these image regions, and less coding is required. Using tools such as motion-prediction and motion-compensation the prediction I done along with P-frames, One I-frame which are included by a typical group of pictures (or "GOP") which is intra-coded. From I- and P-frames additional B-frames are then extrapolated. The: IB-B-P-B-B-I-B-B-P-B-B-I-B-B-P-B-B-I-B-B-P-B-B-I is the typical long-GOP MPEG structure for a 25 frame sequence.

The I-,P-, B- are the three frames and their formation is involved in the MPEG-4 compression. As reference frames and I- frames and the predicted frames are I-, P-, B- frames. Using the technique intraframe the coding of I-frames is performed, without referring to any other frames the reconstruction of these frames are possible. The forwarded prediction is a technique called inter frame technique and by using this the P- frames are coded. From the recent I-frame or P- frame they are forward to reconstruct the B-frames which are necessity of two other frames. Hence, the key frames in the MPEG-4 compression are I frames. In predictive coding by the encoder one can use the multiple feedbacks so that coding performance can be improved. For embedding the data in every I-frame the luminance component (Y) is chosen. The data is embedded and the quantized DCT coefficients is got when in an I frame the 8x8 block of a luminance component(Y) is chosen. Note that in figure 1 the only steps of interest are presented in MPEG-4 compression.

Compression Performance

Subjective, for MPEG-4 mathematically lossless compression and visually lossless compression is defined, but for the standard it is not a requirement. Between lossless compression and lossy compression an important difference is given and highlighted by this original scope statement. These systems are also known as “pseudo lossless”.

Temporal and spatial compression Here, file sizes can grow very rapidly because digital video is the combination of images (sometimes) and audio track and the user is allowed to choose to compress more than once by most video capture and editing software: while digitizing, editing, and the final result is save. Since a loss of quality is brought by each compression potentially and it is best for the last step to save compression. If possible, with little or no compression digitize and edit your video. Two techniques are used by Digital video compression: spatial and temporal compression. In the section on digital images spatial compression was introduced. The removing or reordering of information about a field of colored pixels is involved in it so that file space can be conserved. Temporal compression, as the name suggests, that it operates across time. Instead of saving the information about each frame into the digital video file, the adjoining frame compares the information about the differences between frames (frame differencing) is saved. On periodic key frames are compressed, that it will received on another. The entire still image is saved at each key frame and for frame differencing these complete pictures is used. When compressing digital video another key concept is introduced (but also used with other time-based media, such as audio) called data rate. Data rate refers to the speed at which information must be read from the delivery source. The user is allowed to specify a data rate by most applications when compressing video, so that playback will be smooth for users on, for example, a 56 Kb/second modem.

3.6.3 Frame types [79]

For video compression, the image-to-image prediction is the basic principle involved. An I-frame is the first image and is self-contained, outside of that image there is no dependency. As a reference, the frames following the I frames may use the information. An P-frame (image) is defined as an image which is predicted from one reference frame(image) and an B-frame(image) is defined as an image which is predicted bi-directionally from two reference frames.

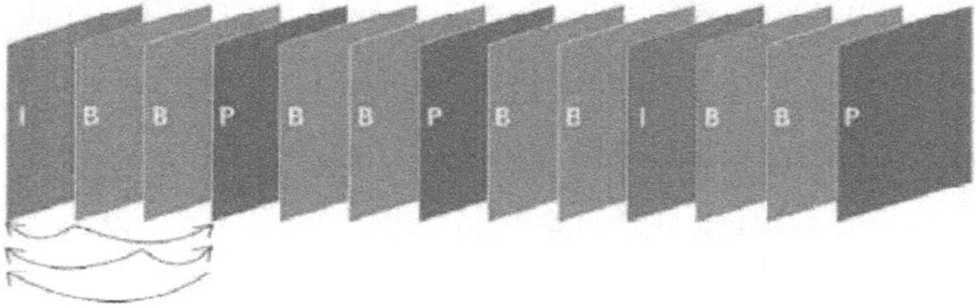

Fig: 3.4: A typical sequence containing I, B, and P frames

Note that a preceding I- or P-frame is referred by P-frame, while both preceding and succeeding I- and P-frames are referred by B-frame as shown in figure in 3.4.

- I-frames: Intra predicted, self-contained.
- P-frames: Predicted from last I or P reference frame
- B-frames: Bidirectional; From two references this is predicted one in the past and one in the future.

When the bit stream frame is decoded by frame then the video decoder restores the video. With an I-frame the decoding must always start, which can be decoded independently, while with current reference image(s) the P- and B frames must be decoded together.

I-frames: As reference or key frames the intra (I) frames are known, where all the necessary data is contained in it to create a complete image. In the group of pictures without requiring data from other frames an I-frame can stand by itself. One I-frame is contained by every group of picture, although it does not have to be the first frame of the group of picture. In MPEG frame the largest type of frame is I-frames, and when compared to different types of MPEG frames they can be decompressed faster.

P-frames: On the basis of closest preceding I or P-frame from the “predicted” picture Predicted (P) frames are encoded. In the form of reference frames the P-frames are known. Than the I-frames the much smaller frames are P-frames.

B-frames: The interpolation from I- and P-frames leads to the encoding of the bi-directional (B) frames. Very little space is required by B-frames, but to decompress longer time is needed because it depends on frames and also some on other frames they depend.

3.6.4 Prediction [79]

With respect to themselves these frames are encoded. Blocks of 8x8 pixels each frame is composed and with respect to themselves they are encoded and to the block of transformation process they are sent directly.

From a past frame-I or frame-P using motion compensated prediction these frames are encoded. In the past reference I or P frame and the current frame, between a 16x16 pixels region (macro block) a prediction error is calculated. The value and direction of the prediction need to be determined by the calculation of motion vector. For P-pictures only one motion vector will be calculated for the sequences of progressive and interlaced. Two motion vectors will be calculated for interlace sequences with field-coding. To 8x8 pixels blocks the prediction error is then composed and to the block transformation it is sent.

Using motion these are pictures encoded and the predictions are compensated from a past and/or future frame-I or frame-P. In the current, past as well as future reference frame-I or frame-P between a 16x16 pixels region a prediction error is calculated. There is a calculation of two motion vectors among them, the value and direction of the forward prediction are determined by using one vector value and direction of the backward prediction are determined by another vector. Four motion vectors will thus be calculated for field-coding frames in interlaced sequences.

It should be noted that as a prediction picture B-picture can never be used. For the best predictor the motion vectors as well as the search areas calculating method are left where by the encoder need to be determined.

3.6.5 Overview of MPEG-4 encoding format [79,86]

- For the purpose of compressing the audio and visual data we use the standard MPEG-4. For video conversation, CD distribution, broadcast television and streaming media, the MPEG-4 standard is used. To incorporate features of MPEG-1, MPEG-2 the MPEG-4 is used.
- The still developing standard is MPEG-4 and into several parts it is divided. The concept of "profiles" and "levels," are included in the standard.
- The massive video files are crunched into pieces by MPEG-4 so that is the reason why they are sent over mobile networks. Because of these blurry pictures millions of people are unwillingly upgrading their mobile phones and for future it works better.
- The interactive features that are offered by MPEG-4 are more important. Similar to Web page the video function looks like and on the screen it allows the people to interact with it.
- The video or images and other types of content are bundled into a file by MPEG-4. To play the special software is required by these files.
- The interactivity of the video may be allowed by MPEG-4. From the rest of the video in a separate layer there is existence of the character, a ball in a sporting event, a rocket ship in a science-fiction epic these all are the individual elements of an video.

3.7 DATA EMBEDDING PROCESS OF RDH_NZAC

Into non-zero AC coefficients of quantized DCT blocks, the data can be embedded. For embedding as shown in Figure 3.3 [34] the sets D_k $(1 \le k \le 9)$ are considered. If $x = d_{k,p}$, here $1 \le p \le K(k)$, use the following f, S, g functions where to embed the bit f is used, for the purpose of extracting the data bit S is used and for the restoration of coefficients g is used.

$$
f(x) = \begin{cases} x + 1 & \text{if } x \ge 2, \\ x - 1 & \text{if } x \le -2, \\ x & \text{if } x = \pm 1 \text{ and } s = 1, \\ x + 1 & \text{if } x = 1 \text{ and } s = 0, \\ x - 1 & \text{if } x = -1 \text{ and } s = 0, \\ 0 & \text{if } x = 0. \end{cases} \quad (3.1)
$$

Where s is the data bit in $\mathbb{I}$ to be embedded.

$$
s(x) = \begin{cases} 1 & \text{if } x = \pm 1, \\ 0 & \text{if } x = \pm 2, \\ \perp & \text{Otherwise.} \end{cases} \quad (3.2)
$$

$$
g(x) = \begin{cases} x - 1 & \text{if } x \ge 2, \\ x + 1 & \text{if } x \le -2, \\ x & \text{if } x = \pm 1, \\ 0 & \text{if } x = 0. \end{cases} \quad (3.3)
$$

The following conditions are satisfied by these functions:

1) $|x - x'| \le 1$. 2) For all x; $(x) = x' \Rightarrow (x') = x$.

3) For all x; from the set {0, 1} or the symbol ⊥ a bit is output of the function (x), which indicates that in x no bit can be embedded.

For the above proposed method the algorithm is presented. To MPEG-4 encoder as an input F is given during the compression. As the sequence of I-, P-, -*frames* the frames of F are expressed by MPEG-4 encoder. For the purpose of embedding the data bits the set of I-frames are considered.

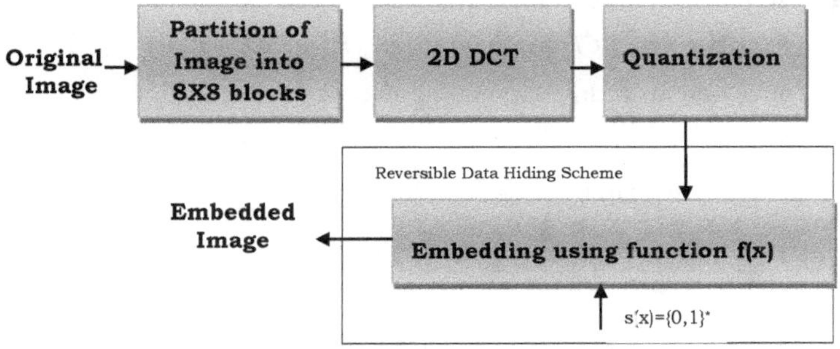

Fig: 3.5: Embedding process of RDH_NZAC

From the figure 3.5 the embedding process, presents RDH technique referred as NZAC. It is designed to achieve better embedding capacity and visual quality in NZAC embedding process, which embeds secret data into quantized DCT coefficients and it has following operations steps shown in figure 3.5

1) Partition of original image I of size M×N is done. 2) Apply 2D DCT 3) Perform for the result obtained in first step quantization 4) The secret data is embedded into Non-zero coefficients of DCT using the function f() to get the resultant embedded Image.

3.7.1 Data Embedding Algorithm of RDH_NZAC

Input : $I = \{I_1, I_2, \ldots, I_m\}$ be the set of I-frames and 𝕀 be the data to be embedded.

Output: The set of $I\text{-}frames$ with embedded data.

forall the $I_i \in I$ do

Extract the Y_i from I_i

Partition $Y_i \rightarrow \{Bi_1, \cdots ,\}$

for each $Bi_j \in Y_i$, where $1 \leq j \leq l$ do

Find the DCT of : $\hat{}Bi_j = DCT(Bi_j)$;

Quantize the DCT coefficients in $\hat{}Bi_j$ as below:

for $i_1 \leftarrow 1$ to 8 do

for $i_2 \leftarrow 1$ to 8 do

$(i_1, i_2) = \hat{}(i_1, i_2)/Q(i_1, i_2)$;

end

end

Consider $(1 \leq k \leq 9)$ sets of Cj as shown in Figure 3.3;

If $x = dk$, where $1 \leq p \leq (k)$, embed the bit s from 𝕀 using the function f shown in equation 3.1

Let the resultant block be C' ;

end

Combine all the $C'j$ blocks into $\hat{C}_i$:$\hat{C}_i \leftarrow \{C'_1, C'_2, \cdots , C'_l\}$;

Restore the $\hat{C}_i$ back to $I_i = \{\hat{C}_i, C_{ib}, C_{ir}\}$;

end

3.8 Data Extraction Process of RDH_NZAC

The data extraction is an inverse process of data embedding. Extract the data bits using the functions s() and restore the modified coefficients using the function g(). The data extraction and restoration is presented in Algorithm 2. We can prove that the proposed scheme is reversible by showing the function f() is invertible to the function g().

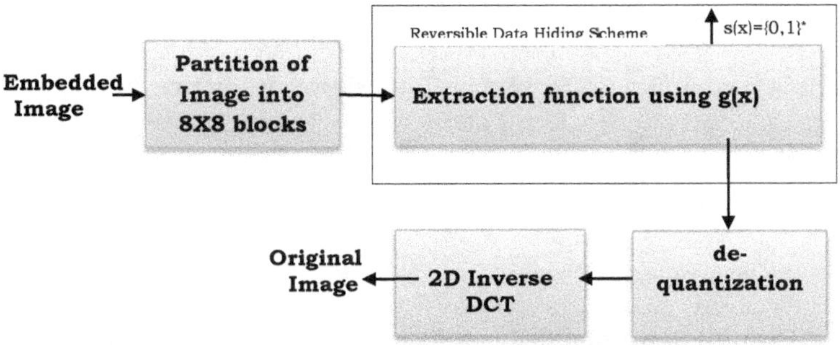

Fig: 3.6: Extraction process of RDH_NZAC

From the figure 3.6 the Extraction procedure, presents RDH technique referred as NZAC. To achieve better embedding capacity, visual quality it is designed.

In NZAC Extraction process, extracts the secret data from the quantized DCT coefficients and it has following operations steps shown in figure 3.6

1) Partition of embedded image I of size M×N is done. 2) Using the function g() from the Non-zero coefficients of DCT the secret data is extracted 3) apply the de-quantization for resultant of third step 4)Inverse DCT to be applied to get the resultant original/restored image.

3.8.1 Data Extraction Algorithm of RDH_NZAC

Input : I, the set of *I-frames* with embedded data.

Output: The set of restored *I-frames*, and the extracted data:'

for all the $I_i \in I$ do

Extract the Ĉ from I_i ;

Partition $\hat{C}^i \rightarrow \{C'_1, C'_2, \cdots, C'_l\}$;

for each $C'_j \in \hat{C}^i$ do

Consider $(1 \leq k \leq 9)$ sets of C'_j as shown in Figure 3.3;

begin

If $x = d_k$, where $1 \leq p \leq (k)$, extract the data bits using the function S shown in equation 3.2;

Restore the modified coefficients using the function g shown in equation 3.3

end

Let the resultant block be E' ;

Dequantize the elements of E'_j as follows ;

for $i_1 \leftarrow 1$ to 8 do

for $i_2 \leftarrow 1$ to 8 do

$R_j\ (i_1, i_2) = E'_j\ (i_1, i_2) \times (i_1, i_2)$;

end

end

$R'_j = IDCT(R_j)$;

end

Combine all the R'_j blocks to get the $\hat{R}_i$

$\hat{R}_i \leftarrow \{R'_1, R'_2, \cdots, R'_l\}$;

Restore the $\hat{R}i$ back to $Ii = \{\hat{R}_i, C_{ib}, C_{ir}\}$;

end

3.9 RESULTS AND ANALYSIS

The MissAm, Akiyo, CarPhone, SalesMan, etc are shown which includes the use of various QCIF formatted videos. In Figure 3.7 & 3.8 some of the test videos are shown, are four original I- frame test videos and four Embedded I- frame test videos. The 176 × 144 pixels is the frame size of all these test videos. By the standard MPEG-4 encoder we compress these test videos.

(a) MissAm

(b) Akiyo

(c) CarPhone

(d) SalesMan

Fig: 3.7: The four original I frames of various test videos

(a) MissAm (b) Akiyo

(c) CarPhone (d) SalesMan

Fig: 3.8: The embedded I frames of test videos

Table 3.2: Comparison of Embedded capacity of C-C Chen Scheme and RDH_NZAC scheme for various test videos

Video Sequence	C-C Chen Scheme	RDH_NZAC Scheme
	Embedded Capacity	Embedded Capacity
MissAm	779	767
Akiyo	1109	1460
CarPhone	1571	1744
SalesMan	1907	2545

The Table 3.2 represent embedded capacity of C-C Chen and RDH_NZAC scheme. The proposed embedded capacity is improved for different test videos because for embedding the data which are more in number the coefficients are utilized.

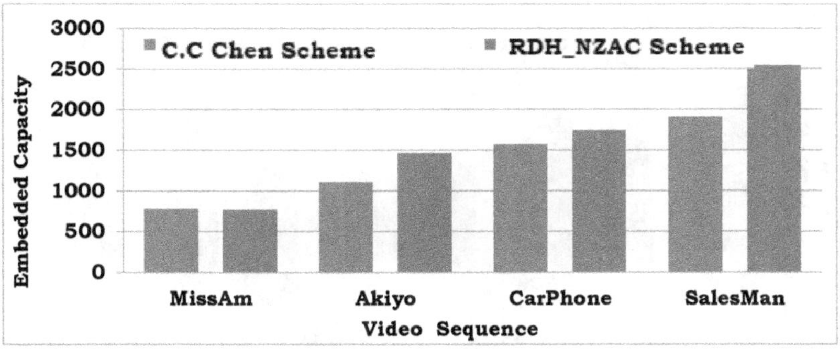

Fig 3.9: Embedded capacity values of C-C Chen scheme and RDH_NZAC scheme

The embedding capacity is represented in figure 3.9. In the figure X-axis input video sequences and Y-axis defines embedding capacity. This graph it can be observed that embedding capacity is dominating in RDH by considering NZAC coefficients in embedding. The embedding capacity is improved better than C-C Chen scheme.

Table 3.3: Comparison of PSNR for C-C Chen Scheme and RDH_NZAC scheme for various test videos

Video Sequence	C-C Chen Scheme	RDH_NZAC Scheme
	PSNR	PSNR
MissAm	34.3489	37.0801
Akiyo	31.5554	33.5383
CarPhone	30.1427	32.2726
SalesMan	29.0330	31.4584

From the table 3.3 it is observed that proposed PSNR values are improved more than the C-C Chen scheme. This is because the alterations to the coefficients is minimized by our design and for embedding the data utilize coefficients , whose number is more.

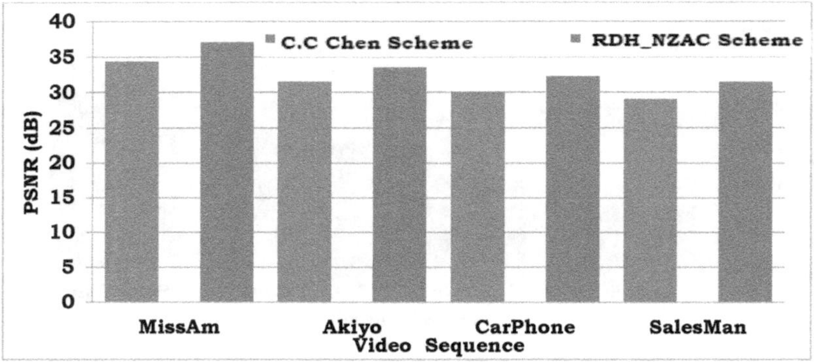

Fig 3.10: PSNR values of C-C Chen and RDH_NZAC scheme

In figure 3.10 X-axis defines input video sequence and Y-axis defines PSNR. In this figure 3.10 it is observed that RDH_NZAC scheme PSNR values are more dominating than C-C Chen scheme.

Table 3.4: Comparison of PSNRM values for C-C Chen and RDH_NZAC scheme for various test videos

Video Sequence	C-C Chen Scheme	RDH_NZAC Scheme
	PSNRM	PSNRM
Miss Am	32.3898	34.9831
Akiyo	32.1918	32.9557
Car Phone	31.6978	32.6588
Sales Man	31.3962	31.1866

From the table 3.4 it can be observed that PSNRM values are more than the C-C Chen Scheme.

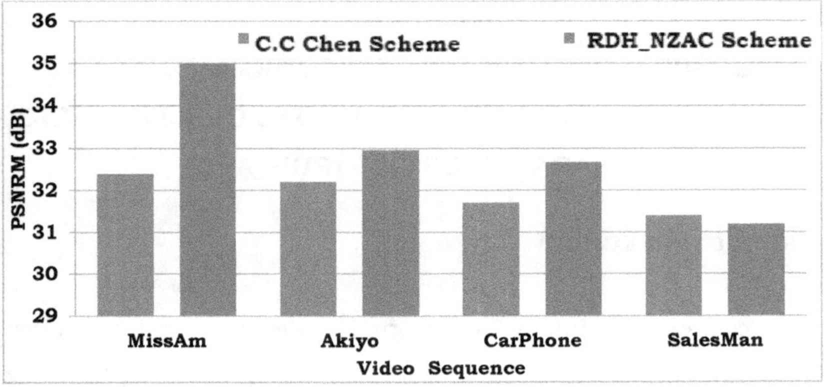

Fig: 3.11 PSNRM values of C-C Chen and RDH_NZAC scheme

In figure 3.11 X-axis defines input video sequence and Y-axis defines PSNRM. In this figure 3.11 it can be observed that PSNRM i.e., visual quality values are improved better than the C-C Chen scheme. Which takes into account the sensitivity of human eyes to distortion in high, low spatial frequencies and the masking effects given as follows?

$$\text{PSNR-HVS-M} = 10\log_{10}\frac{255^2}{MSE^{HVS-M}}, (dB)$$

Where between the original, embedded (distorted) luminance

components the $MSEHV\ S{-}M$ [9] is computed.

3.10 SUMMARY

When the data is embedded in DCT domain, the modifications to the cover content need to be minimal for achieving reversibility. This results into a better tradeoff between the visual quality and embedding capacity. The proposed scheme improves both the visual quality and the embedding capacity.

Chapter - 4

A REVERSIBLE DATA EMBEDDING SCHEME FOR GRAY SCALE IMAGES TO AUGMENT THE VISUAL QUALITY USING HVS CHARACTERISTICS (RDH_AVQ)

4.1 INTRODUCTION TO DCT

In image compression, the DCT transform is widely used and it is widely accepted in multimedia standards and it is an orthogonal transformation. The attempt is made so that the data of image can be de-correlated by Discrete Cosine Transform (DCT). Without losing efficiency of compression like other transforms the coefficient of each transform can be independently encoded after de-correlation.

For the 1-D sequence having length N is the most common definition of DCT is

$$C(u,v) = \propto (u) \sum_{x=0}^{N-1} f(x) \cos\left[\frac{\pi(2x+1)u}{2N}\right] \quad (4.1)$$

CWhere u = 0, 1, 2, ….., N −1 & f(x) a original signal to be transformed and the inverse transform is defined as which is given below

$$f(x) = \sum_{u=0}^{N-1} \propto (u) C(u) \cos\left[\frac{\pi(2x+1)u}{2N}\right] \quad (4.2)$$

Where $u = 0,1,2,\ldots,N-1$, $C(u)$ is transformed coefficient and $\propto = (u)\ is$ defined below.

$$\propto(u) = \begin{cases} \sqrt{\frac{1}{N}} & for\ u = 0 \\ \sqrt{\frac{2}{N}} & for\ u \neq 0. \end{cases}$$

For u=0, 1-D DCT, $when\ u = 0, C(u) = \sqrt{\frac{1}{N}} \sum_{x=0}^{N-1} f(x)$. Thus, the sample sequence average value is the first transform coefficient. As DC *Coefficient it known* in literature. The *AC Coefficients are* remaining coefficients.

The 2D DCT is expressed as

$$C(u,v) = \propto(u) \propto(v) \sum_{x=0}^{N-1}\sum_{y=0}^{N-1} f(x,y) \cos\left[\frac{\pi(2x+1)u}{2N}\right] \cos\left[\frac{\pi(2x+1)v}{2N}\right] \qquad (4.3)$$

Where $f(x,y)$ is a 2-D signal (image) and $C(u,v)$ is a 2-D DCT transform signal and $u, v = 0,1,2, \ldots, N-1$ and $=\propto(u)$ and $\propto(v)$ are defined below.

$$\propto(u) = \begin{cases} \sqrt{\frac{1}{N}} & for\ u = 0 \\ \sqrt{\frac{2}{N}} & for\ u \neq 0. \end{cases}$$

The below equation describes the inverse transform

$$f(x,y) = \sum_{u=0}^{N-1}\sum_{v=0}^{N-1} \propto(u) \propto(v)\, C(u,v) \cos\left[\frac{\pi(2x+1)u}{2N}\right] \cos\left[\frac{\pi(2x+1)v}{2N}\right] \qquad (4.4)$$

Where $f(x,y)$ is the restored signal and $x, y = 0,1,2, \ldots, N-1$. The basis function of 2D is generated when set of the same functions of vertically orientated one are multiplied with the basis function of 1D horizontally oriented function.

4.1.2 DCT Properties

In the previous sections a mathematical foundation for DCT has been discussed. Though, the study of image processing application has not been studied. Some properties of DCT are outlined by this section and to image processing applications these are of specific values.

Decorrelation

Between neighbouring pixels, the removal of redundancy is the major advantage of image transformation. This show how the transform coefficients are uncorrelated which can be encoded independently. At all lags after the DCT process the autocorrelation amplitude is very small. Hence, the excellent de-correlation properties which are exhibited by DCT are indicated by it.

Energy Compaction

For images of highly correlated the excellent energy compaction is exhibited by DCT. In the reconstructed image without introducing visual distortion the coefficients with relatively small amplitudes is abandoned by the quantizer according to the property just mentioned. As few coefficients as possible with the input data which can be packed and because of it's ability transformation scheme efficiency we can determine directly.

Separability

As shown below the transform of DCT can be expressed,

$$C(u,v) = \propto(u) \propto(v) \sum_{x=0}^{N-1} \sum_{y=0}^{N-1} f(x,y) \cos\left[\frac{\pi(2x+1)u}{2N}\right] \cos\left[\frac{\pi(2x+1)v}{2N}\right] \quad (4.5)$$

Where $f(x,y)$ is a 2-D signal (image) and $C(u,v)$ is a 2-D DCT transform signal and and $u,v = 0,1,2,\dots,N-1$. In an image rows and columns are introduced by consecutive 1D operations and performs in two steps primary operation and produce $C(u,v)$. This property is known as separability.

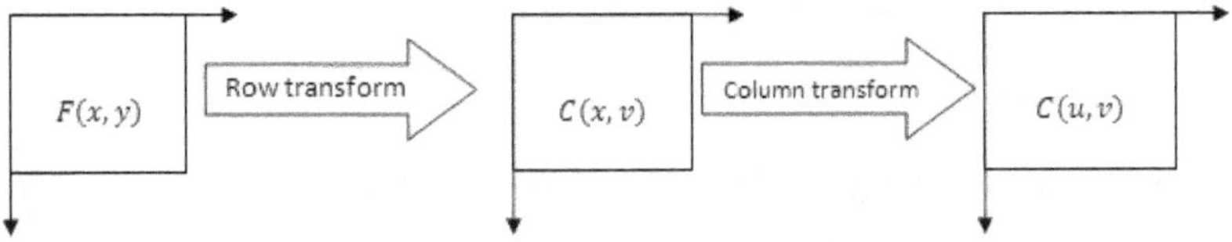

Fig: 4.1: 2D DCT Computation using separability property

Symmetry

The operations of row and column are functionally identical which is resulted in the above equation. It is the symmetric transformation is defined as

$$T = AfA \qquad (4.6)$$

With entries $\propto (i,j)$ the symmetric transformation of A of order N x N is specified by

$$\propto (i,j) = \propto (j) \sum_{j=0}^{N-1} \cos\left[\frac{\pi(2j+1)}{2N}\right] \qquad (4.7)$$

and f is the image matrix $N \times N$

it is an extremely very useful property. This property is useful to the images and it also implies that the transformation matrix can be pre-computed offline.

Orthogonality

Let us inverse the transformation which is denoted as T =so that the ideas which are discussed in the preceding section can be extended

$$f = A^{-1}TA^{-1} \tag{4.8}$$

The basic functions of DCT are orthogonal. Hence, the statement $A^{-1} = A^T$ states that the transpose of A is equal to the inverse transformation matrix. Therefore, the addition to its de-correlation characteristics, in the pre-computation complexity some reduction is rendered by Orthogonality.

4.2 QUANTIZATION

The discrete signal range is formulated by Quantizations, so that only a discrete is considered by the quantized signal. As the quantized signal the distortion is introduced which cannot be eliminated. It is seen that exact reconstruction is possible in quantization under suitable conditions which is different from sampling where quantization is generally irreversible where loss of information is resulted.

The discrete quantization levels number is used in quantization. For the purpose of representing each sample need the quality of resulting signal versus the amount of data and it is the basic trade-off in this choice. For the purpose of representing L levels, the $N = log_2 L$ bits are needed to represent, we can represent $L = 2^N$ levels for different levels or conversely with N bits.

A sample is autonomous of other samples in this quantizing. Utilizing some limited number of bits which are individualistic of the location for images or sample time and independent of surrounding sample values signal amplitude is basically represented. The entire process is represented when the mapping takes between the variable amplitude x to a quantization levels having discrete levels $\{r_1, r_2..., r_L\}$.

Relationship with certain values of t_k or on simple thresholding the mapping is regularly based. The levels of transition or decision are known as t_k, and the reconstruction levels represented as r_k . To r_k the x gets mapped when the amplitude signal x is between t_k and t_{k+1} . In the simplest zero memory quantizer the transition and the reconstruction levels are uniformly spaced. In addition, the contouring or false contouring are shown which are aircrafts. These refer the artificial boundaries and they become visible because of the large and unexpected intensity changes which takes place between consecutive gray levels.

Due to quantization with about 256 amplitude levels or 8 bits per sample the distortion or noise in the audio signal can be heard.

It is expected that depending upon the quantizer the distortion amount be demonstrated in non-uniform quantization and therefore the distortion can be minimized when a good quantizer is chosen. With the values of the transition and reconstruction levels the quantizer is designed and it is the only choice in designing the zero memory quantizer when the number of levels is fixed (or bits per sample). By blindly taking the levels which are uniformly spaced its better when a good quantization levels are chosen. For example, on a certain range of gray levels if an image is never taken then it seen that in this range of gray levels there is no question of wasting quantization levels. In a more efficient way one can represent the image if the gray levels are finely represented by quantization levels. However, for the optimum quantizer in general, the equations are too difficult to solve analytically.

The values have been tabulated for the purpose of optimal quantization and reconstruction levels so that the equations are solved numerically. For the optimal quantizer various approximations and suboptimal alternatives have been developed. The better results can be obtained from the sub-optimal than the simple uniform quantization. If a particular image the quantization levels are chosen to be tailored then the reconstruction levels need to be stored while storing the image by doing this the image is properly displayed. This suffers a certain amount of overhead, so that for each image a different quantizer can be chosen. Instead, for working a certain class of images the quantization levels are chosen and in a given application they are expected to be encountered. Such issues decrease with decreasing cost of memory and communication and increasing capacity.

The properties of human perception are involved so that a non-uniform quantization levels may be chosen in a different rationale. The Weber's law is satisfied by many human perceptual attributes and it states that rather than in absolute changes to the proportional changes in the amplitude of a stimulus we are sensitive. For example, in case of vision, to *contrast* humans are sensitive but not to absolute luminance and to the ambient luminance level our contrast sensitivity is proportional, Thus for lower luminance levels as well as there is no need that gray levels to be spaced close together for extremely bright luminance levels. Therefore, with respect to contrast sensitivity it is quantized uniformly, and to luminance it is logarithmically related. A number of reasons are provided by this for picking up the logarithmic quantization levels which are spaced equally. With this choice for even approximating any "optimal" quantizer there are no claims in general. The reason why the optimal quantizer is ignored is that what is visually pleasing it does correspond to minimize the mean square error every time.

4.2.1 Quantization Tables

On JPEG compression quality there is a greater influence of quantization table. The degree of compression achieved is influenced by it. For the DCT values to provide the greatest number of bits there is a development of these tables (by trial and error), which are seen mostly and to the human vision system it had great impact.

In an 8 × 8 array for DCT output the table of quantization is applied. The DC coefficient are the upper most one, and the 63 AC coefficients are the remaining ones, as one moves rightward and downward in horizontal and vertical frequencies there is increment. As to lower frequencies the eye of human is sensitive, for the DCT coefficients of upper and leftmost ones the more bits and quantization in minimum quantity is used where in the vertical and horizontal directions the lower frequencies are present.

As shown below in the JPEG standard the example baseline tables are contained in it and in vertical and horizontal directions.

Table 4.1: Baseline tables provided in the JPEG standard

16	11	10	16	24	40	51	61
12	12	14	19	26	58	60	55
14	13	16	24	40	57	69	56
14	17	22	29	51	87	80	62
18	22	37	56	68	109	103	77
24	35	55	67	81	104	113	92
49	64	78	87	103	121	120	101
72	92	95	98	112	100	103	99

Quantization table for luminance component

17	18	24	47	99	99	99	99
18	21	26	66	99	99	99	99
24	26	56	99	99	99	99	99
47	66	99	99	99	99	99	99
99	99	99	99	99	99	99	99
99	99	99	99	99	99	99	99
99	99	99	99	99	99	99	99
99	99	99	99	99	99	99	99

Quantization table for chrominance component

For various JPEG versions the tables of quantization are developed and to the human visual system it has greater visualization. For the output $B_{j,k}$ there are few possible values if $Q_{j,k}$ is large. This can be explained well with an example. If the quantization value is 99 the −1, 0, or +1 are the rounded output values. When the values of j or k is 3 or larger then to zero $B_{j,k}$ will be rounded which indicates the image region having little high frequency.

In quantization the loss of data is resulted and the recovery of bit is difficult. To reduce the data having little noticeable impact on the image quality is discarded and by doing this the amount of data is reduced.

In the following manner the computation of quantized DCT coefficients is done:

$B_{j,k} = round\left(\frac{G_{j,k}}{Q_{j,k}}\right)$ for j=0,1,2,......N_1-1; k=0,1,2,...N_2-1

Where the coefficients of unquantized DCT is denoted by G; the quantization matrix shown above is denoted by Q and the quantized DCT coefficients is denoted by B.

$$\begin{pmatrix} -26 & -3 & -6 & 2 & 2 & -1 & 0 & 0 \\ 0 & -2 & -4 & 1 & 1 & 0 & 0 & 0 \\ -3 & 1 & 5 & -1 & -1 & 0 & 0 & 0 \\ -4 & 1 & 2 & -1 & 0 & 0 & 0 & 0 \\ 1 & 0 & 0 & 0 & 0 & 0 & 0 & 0 \\ 0 & 0 & 0 & 0 & 0 & 0 & 0 & 0 \\ 0 & 0 & 0 & 0 & 0 & 0 & 0 & 0 \\ 0 & 0 & 0 & 0 & 0 & 0 & 0 & 0 \end{pmatrix}$$

In the above expression let us place some values for better understanding for example, let the sample value be −415 (the DC coefficient) and to the nearest integer it is rounded.

$$round\left(\frac{-415}{16}\right) = round(-25.9375) = -26$$

4.3 CONTRAST SENSITIVE FUNCTION (CSF)

Contrast Sensitive Function decrease the sensitive by using various frequencies [23]. The stimuli pattern cannot be recognized if the visual stimuli frequency is too high. Imagine the vertical black and white stripes are contained in an image. We will be unable to see individual stripes if the stripes are very thin (i.e. a few thousand per millimetre). All that we will see is a gray image. There is a threshold width if the stripes become wider and wider, from which the stripes can be distinguished. The quantization table JPEG values are normalized and then shared.

At low contrast levels to see the details the ability is provided by Contrast sensitivity. For contrast levels having low values the important thing to remember is the visual information. In communication, the visual information related to facial expression and is carried out by the faint shadows on our faces. The critical low contrast forms can be seen in orientation and mobility, such as the faint shadows, curb, and stairs when walking down. In traffic, at low contrast levels there is a demanding situation, for example, fog, rain, seeing in dusk and snow fall. The tasks like reading and writing are continued without any problem in near vision even though the information is at low contrast. At threshold the contrast reciprocal is the contrast sensitivity. The contrast sensitivity of he/she is high and vice versa.

Because of the difference in luminance the contrast is created. The reflected light amount, reflected from two adjacent surfaces. In slightly different ways it can be defined. The Michelson formula is usually used in clinical work:

$$contrast = \frac{L_{max} - L_{min}}{L_{max} + L_{min}} \qquad (4.9)$$

The definition of Weber contrast also exists:

$$contrast = \frac{L_{max} - L_{min}}{L_{max}} \qquad (4.10)$$

Where on the lighter surface the luminance is given by L_{max} and on the darker surface the luminance is given by L_{min}.

The ratio is 1 when there is no reflected light and when darker surface is black. In the form of percent contrast is usually expressed, and the multiplication of ratio is done by 100. To the maximum contrast, the visual acuity charts symbols are close. To modulate frequencies the CSF is often used for image quality and difference metrics. For this reason, as the Modulation Transfer Function (MTF) the CSF is often erroneously referred. The Barten and Daly, says that which threshold modulation function will perform the contrast sensitivity function which is referred and normalized by the frequency based on equal contrast thresholds.

For image difference calculations generate threshold modulation functions are generated and many models of contrast sensitivity are there. The separable convolution kernels to "blur" out spatial frequencies which cannot be perceived which is used by the spatial pre-processing of the S-CIELAB model. The Movshon, Barten, and Daly models are the CSF models with varying complexities.

Movshon CSF

By Movshon and Kiorpes [73] the simplest contrast sensitivity function which is described and examined here and it is a exponential function of three parameter. In equation 1 the equation form is shown below, where in cycles per degree (CPD) the representation of spatial frequency is given by in f

$$csf(f) = a.f.e^{-b.f} \qquad (4.11)$$

To existing luminance, contrast sensitivity data this equation can be fitted. For *a, b,* and *c* respectively the 75, 0.2, and 0.8 values can be used. For the achromatic contrast sensitivity function the general band-pass shape of desired one is formed by using three parameter equations. The two-dimensional equation form which is used in a color image difference metric. This result is an isotropic function.

Both strengths and weakness are contained by simple form of this model. For all viewing conditions this function is the same, unless to existing data, the parameters are specifically fit. It is assumed that the contrast sensitivity functions are altered by viewing conditions. For luminance level this is the main case where the shape of the contrast sensitivity function is flattening. A more complicated function is necessary to better predict changes in viewing condition.

Barten CSF

For the use in SQRI image quality model by Barten a more complicated model was described for the purpose of contrast sensitivity function. With the human eye's optical MTF there is beginning of contrast sensitivity, and as a Gaussian function it is expressed. With the photon and neural noise, and lateral inhibition models, the modification of MTF is done. As a function of pupil diameter, luminance level, and image size, an isotropic band-pass shape is resulted. The Movshon model design is quite complicated, for varying viewing conditions it possesses greater flexibility. The development and form of this CSF [80] is described in detail by Barten.

4.4 S.GUJJUNOORI SCHEME

In the middle frequency coefficients of DCT embedding, data play important role in data hiding schemes. The ambiguity of same values of coefficients appear after the embedding when the alterations of non-zero coefficients is done during the process of embedding. The more visual distortions are caused to eliminate the ambiguity process. While embedding the data Quantized DCT coefficients are used during embedding. This will avoid ambiguity [78] care must be taken.

4.5 RDH_AVQ SCHEME

With the help of the three consecutive zeroes for an image, the embedding capacity is calculated. A few non-zero values are partially neglected when eliminating ambiguity and while improving in the visual quality. When the use of non-zero coefficients is minimized then there is a improvement in visual quality and in this process a scheme is proposed called reversible data embedding scheme. To Ameliorate Visual Quality (AVQ), the proposed scheme is referred and therefore the visual quality of embedded image may be improved by this scheme. For embedding the data a gray scale's image middle frequency quantized DCT coefficients are considered as shown in Figure 4.2.

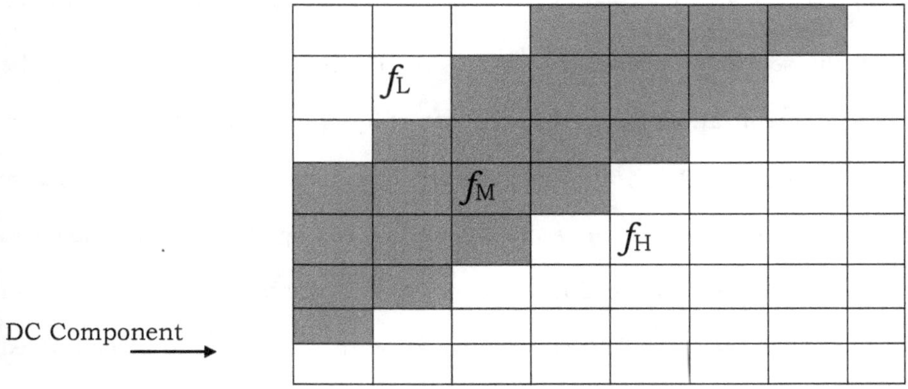

Fig 4.2: DCT Mid frequency region to embed the secret data (f_M)

f_L –DCT Low frequency regions f_M-DCT Mid frequency regions

f_H-DCT High frequency regions

-13	-8	-2	-1	-1	0	0	0	
12	0	-5	-1	-1	0	0	0	
0	9	-4	-2	1	-1	-1	0	
1	3	0	-3	0	0	0	0	h_8
1	0	0	0	0	0	0	0	h_6
0	1	0	0	0	0	0	0	h_4
0	0	0	0	0	0	0	0	h_7
0	0	0	0	0	0	0	0	
				h_9	h_7	h_5	h_3	h_1

Fig 4.3: An 8 × 8 DCT quantized block before embedding

Let an image be I and the data which is to be embedded secretly be S. As 8 ×8 blocks the partition of image I of size M×N is done. Using 2D DCT [4] into frequency domain these 8×8 blocks are transformed. The image size be N×N if considered image is a square.

Let $I = \{I_1, I_2, I_3, \dots I_m\}$, where I_j is the jth 8×8 block of I and $m = (N \times N)/64$. Let the set of DCT transformed blocks be $C = \{C_1, C_2, C_3, \dots C_m\}$. Let Q be the 8×8 quantization block. Let the set of quantized DCT blocks of I *be* $CQ = \{CQ_1, CQ_2, CQ_3, \dots, CQ_m\}$. Let the set of embedded blocks of image be $E = \{E_1, E_2, E_3, \dots E_m\}$ be. In every CQ_i for embedding the data as shown in Figure 1 let the sets of middle frequency coefficients be $H = \{h_1, h_2, \dots, h_9\}$. In the mid of three ceaseless consecutive zeros the data need to be embedded which is present nearby either a non-zero coefficient or at the end of sets considered.

-13	-8	-2	-1	-1	0	0	0	
12	0	-5	-1	-1	0	0	0	
0	9	-4	-2	1	-1	-1	0	
1	3	0	-3	0	0	0	0	h_8
1	0	0	1	0	0	0	0	h_6
0	1	1	0	0	0	0	0	
0	0	0	0	0	0	0	0	h_4
0	0	0	0	0	0	0	0	h_2
				h_9	h_7	h_5	h_3	h_1

Fig 4.4: An 8×8 DCT quantized block after embedding

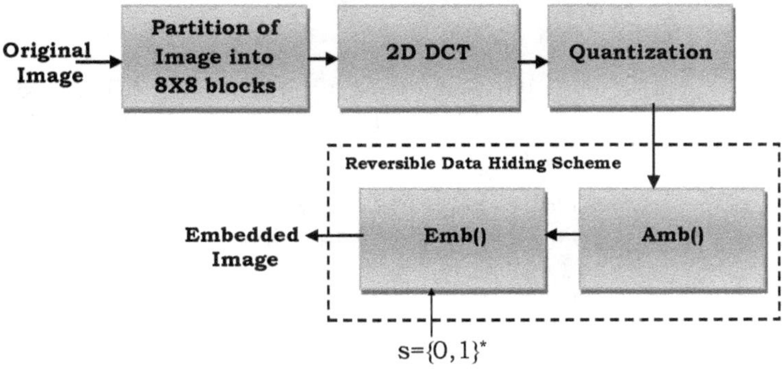

Fig 4.5: Embedding process of RDH_AVQ

4.5.1 Data Embedding Process of RDH_AVQ

In middle frequency coefficients the data is embedded when the sets are considered where the condition of having three consecutive zeroes is satisfied from high to low frequency as shown in figure. The use of non-zero values is minimized in the process of elimination of ambiguity, therefore in the visual quality there is an improvement. The functions, Amb and Emb are used by the data embedding procedure. Before embedding the ambiguity need to be eliminated if not for this purpose Amb is used so that in advance the ambiguity is eliminated so that there will be no problems. From high frequency to low frequency the continuous sequence of quantized DCT coefficients is denoted by tuple (a_h,a_m,a_l). For the coefficients having middle frequency as in (5) to embed the data the function Emb is used, where the random secret data is denoted by s = {0, 1}* and from high frequency to low frequency the tuple of sequence of quantized DCT coefficients is denoted by (a'_h , a'_m, a'_l) after eliminating the ambiguity where in the mid of three consecutive zeroes, the secret data s is embedded as in (5) and the tuple containing the embedded data is denoted by (e_h, e_m, e_l).

In the algorithm of data embedding is shown.

$$(a_h^{'}, a_m^{'}, a_l^{'}) = Amb(a_h, a_m, a_l) = \begin{cases} (a_h, a_m + 1, a_l) & if\ (a_h = 0, a_m = 1, a_l = 0) \\ (a_h, a_m, a_l) & otherwise \end{cases} \quad (4)$$

$$(e_h, e_m, e_l) = Emb((a_h, a_m, a_l), s) = \begin{cases} (a_h, s, a_l) & if\ (a_h = 0, a_m = 0, a_l = 0) \\ (a_h^{'}, a_m^{'}, a_l^{'}) & otherwise \end{cases} \quad (5)$$

Where a secret bit 0 or 1 is denoted by s

4.5.2 Data embedding algorithm of RDH_AVQ

Step 1: Let the cover image be I and s = {0, 1}*

Step 2: In to 8 × 8 blocks the image I is partitioned, $I = \{I_1, I_2, I_3, \ldots, I_m\}$

Step 3: On every 8 × 8 block apply 2D DCT, k

```
for i = 1 to 8
    for j = 1 to 8
        Ck(i,j) = DCT (Ik(i,j)) ;
    end
end
```

For an 8 × 8 blocks the transformed set of DCT be $C = \{C_1, C_2, C_3, \ldots, C_m\}$

Step 4: Apply quantization on every transformed 8 × 8 block, k for i = 1 to 8

for j = 1 to 8

$CQ_k(i, j) = C_k(i, j)/Q(i, j);$

end

end

The set of DCT quantized 8 × 8 blocks be $CQ = \{CQ_1, CQ_2, CQ_3, \ldots, CQ_m\}$

Step 5: For the purpose of embedding the data the $h_i (1 < i < 9)$ be the set of middle frequency coefficients. Before embedding, eliminate the ambiguity in Every 8 × 8 block using equation (4)

Step 6: for each $I_j \in I$ Let in the set h_i the number of ceaseless zeroes denoted by c_{h_i} from high to low frequency

$|h_i|$ denotes the size of h_i.

if $(c_{h_i} \geq \left\lceil \frac{|h_i|}{2} \right\rceil - 1)$

Embed the data using the function Emb in (5)

endif

endfor

Step 7: Let E_i be an embedded block. Combine all the embedded blocks into

$E = \{E_1, E_2, E_3, \ldots E_m\}$.

4.5.3 Data Extraction Process of RDH_AVQ

The process of embedding data in reverse process is called data extraction procedure. The *Ext* and *Rest* are the functions which are used by the data extraction procedure. The secret embedded data is extracted by using *Ext,* as in (6), after extracting the original form the data can be restored back by *Rest,* is used as in (7). In Algorithm 2 the extraction procedure of data is shown.

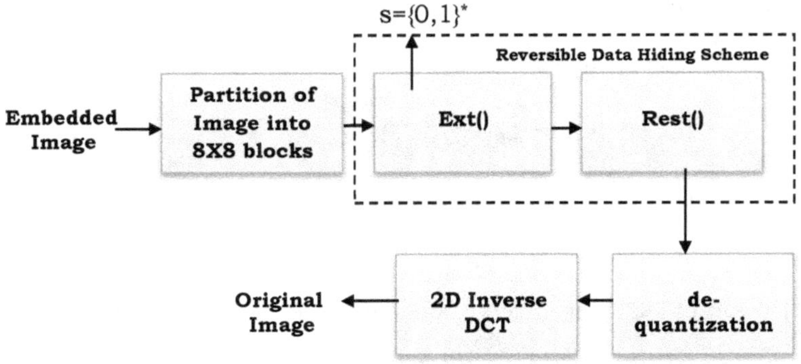

Fig 4.6: Extraction process of RDH_AVQ

$$ex = (ex_h, ex_m, ex_{l\ h}) = Ext(e_h, e_m, e_l)\begin{cases} 0 & if\ (e_h = 0, e_m = 0, e_l = 0) \\ 1 & if\ (e_h = 0, e_m = 1, e_l = 0) \end{cases} \quad (6)$$

$$Rest((ex_h, ex_m, ex_l) = \begin{cases} (ex_h, ex_m - 1, ex_l)\ if\ (ex_h = 0, ex_m = 2, ex_l = 0) \\ (ex_h, ex_m, ex_l) \quad otherwise \end{cases} \quad (7)$$

4.5.4 Data extracting algorithm of RDH_AVQ

Step 1: Let the embedded image be E.

Step 2: As 8×8 blocks the E is partitioned

Step 3: $foreach\ E_j \in E$

Consider $h_i (1 < i < 9)$ be the set of middle frequency coefficients.

$if\ c_{h_i} \geq \left\lceil \frac{|h_i|}{2} \right\rceil - 1$

Extract the data using Ext as in (6).

$endif$

$endfor$

Step 4: After extraction, the restore the coefficients using $Rest$ as in equation (7)

Step 5: Let the extracted image be E'

Step 6: Apply de-quantization on every extracted 8 × 8 block

$for\ i = 1\ to\ 8$

$for\ j\ =\ 1\ to\ 8$

$$R(i,j) = E'(i,j) \times Q(i,j)\ ;$$

end

end

Step 7: Apply $2D\ IDCT$ on every 8 × 8 block

$for\ i = 1\ to\ 8$

$for\ j\ =\ 1\ to\ 8$

$$R'(i,j) = IDCT(R(i,j))\ ;$$

end

end

Step 8: Let R_i' be the restored block and combine all R_i' into

$R' = \{R_1', R_2', R_3', \dots, R_m'\};$

4.6 RESULTS AND ANALYSIS

With the scheme of S. Gujjunoori et. al., [74] the results are compared. In the experiments the image having size of gray scale where images of Elaine, Zelda, Lena, etc are included. In Figure 4.7 the data embedded images is observed. The PSNR, SSIM and SSIM_INDEX are the metrics by using these for degraded images the visual quality is assessed. Here, in an 512 X 512 image the embedding capacity is total number of bits be embedded.

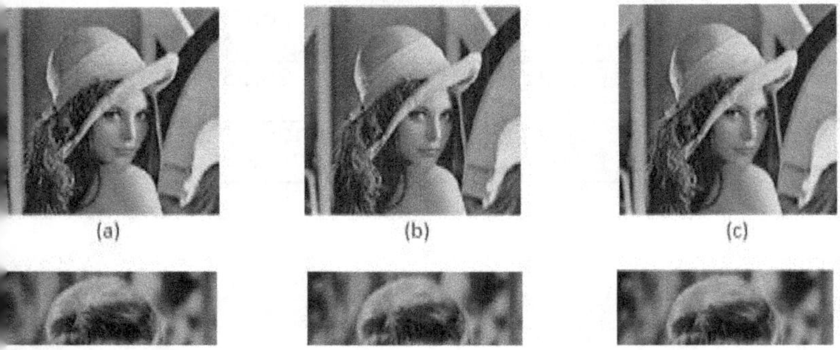

The Lena, Zelda and Elaine's original images are shown in figure 4.6: (a), (d), (g). The data embedded images of respectively Using the scheme of S. Gujjunoori et. al.,. scheme in (b), (e), (h) of figure 4.7 the Lena, Zelda and Elaine's data embedded images are shown. The Lena, Zelda and Elaine's data embedded images are shown in (c), (f), (i) by using proposed scheme.

In visual quality there is an improvement in terms of SSIM_INDEX , SSIM and PSNR, the improvement is measured.

Table 4.2: S. Gujjunoori et.al and RDH_AVQ Scheme PSNR values

Images	PSNR	
	S. Gujjunoori et.al., Scheme	**RDH_AVQ Scheme**
barb512	26.2109	28.4345
airplane	26.3099	28.7784
baboon	26.0568	26.0903
Boat	26.3478	28.3597
elaine	26.3395	28.0532

crowd	26.3236	28.8307
building	26.4371	28.3516
couple512	26.3696	28.4431
goldhill	26.3396	28.3936
parrots	26.7503	28.0405
Lena	26.2535	29.16
plane	26.3004	28.8393
zelda	26.3678	28.7484

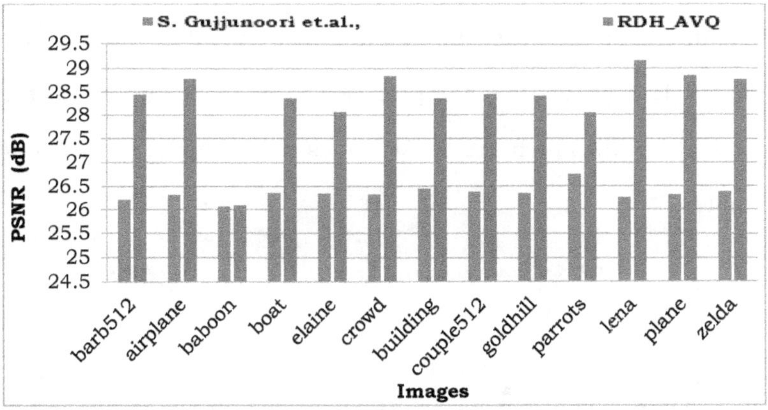

Fig 4.8: Improved visual quality measured in terms of PSNR

Than S.gujjunoori et.al., scheme (blue color) the good results for PSNR is achieved by RDH_AVQ scheme (red color) it is observed in figure 4.8 and from table 4.2.

Table 4.3: S.gujjunoori et.al., and RDH_AVQ Scheme SSIM values

	SSIM		
Images	**S.gujjunoori et.al., Scheme**	**RDH_AVQ Scheme**	**Improved SSIM**
barb512	0.904	0.9341	0.0301

airplane	0.7491	0.8267	0.0776
baboon	0.9388	0.954	0.0152
boat	0.8893	0.9218	0.0325
elaine	0.8683	0.9024	0.0341
crowd	0.9069	0.9366	0.0297
building	0.8814	0.9161	0.0347
couple512	0.8869	0.9202	0.0333
goldhill	0.9007	0.9298	0.0291
parrots	0.8373	0.8645	0.0272
lena	0.8722	0.9132	0.041
plane	0.8373	0.8895	0.0522
zelda	0.8602	0.9055	0.0453

The S.gujjunoori et.al., values of SSIM and the RDH_AVQ scheme are shown in table 4.3. It indicates that the proposed SSIM values improved then the existing values, how much the SSIM values are improved is also shown in above table.

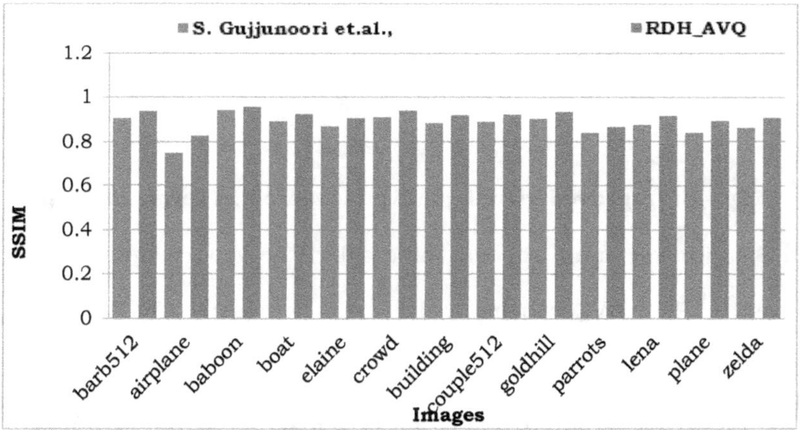

Fig 4.9: Improved visual quality measured in terms of SSIM

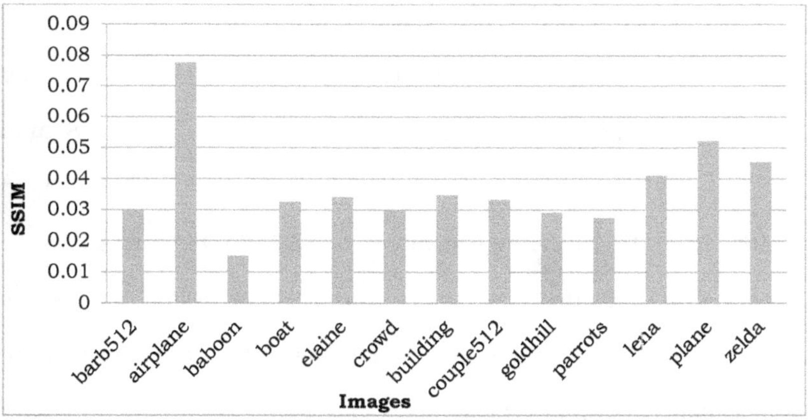

Fig 4.10: Improved SSIM when compared to S.gujjunoori et.al., scheme

When compared with the S.gujjunoori et.al., scheme (blue) which is observed from figure 4.9, there is an improvement in SSIM which is observed from figure 4.10.

Table 4.4: S.gujjunoori et.al., and RDH_AVQ Scheme SSIM_INDEX values

Images	SSIM_INDEX		
	S.gujjunoori et.al., Scheme	RDH_AVQ Scheme	Improved SSIM_INDEX
barb512	0.6479	0.72	0.0721
airplane	0.3822	0.4967	0.1145
baboon	0.7745	0.7913	0.0168
boat	0.5995	0.6683	0.0688
elaine	0.513	0.5732	0.0602
crowd	0.6188	0.7093	0.0905
building	0.6358	0.6996	0.0638
couple512	0.5926	0.6746	0.082
goldhill	0.6072	0.6814	0.0742
parrots	0.5039	0.5489	0.045

lena	0.5685	0.6686	0.1001
plane	0.5144	0.6169	0.1025
zelda	0.4807	0.5886	0.1079

for S.gujjunoori et.al., and the RDH_AVQ scheme the values of SSIM_INDEX are shown in above table 4.4. It indicates that the proposed SSIM_INDEX values are improved then the existing values, how much the SSIM_INDEX values are improved is available in above table.

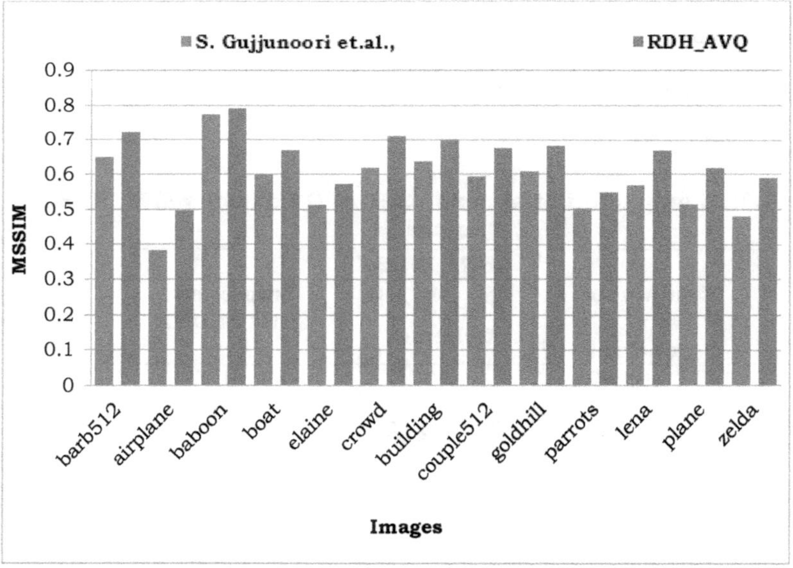

Fig 4.11: Improved visual quality measured in terms of SSIM_INDEX.

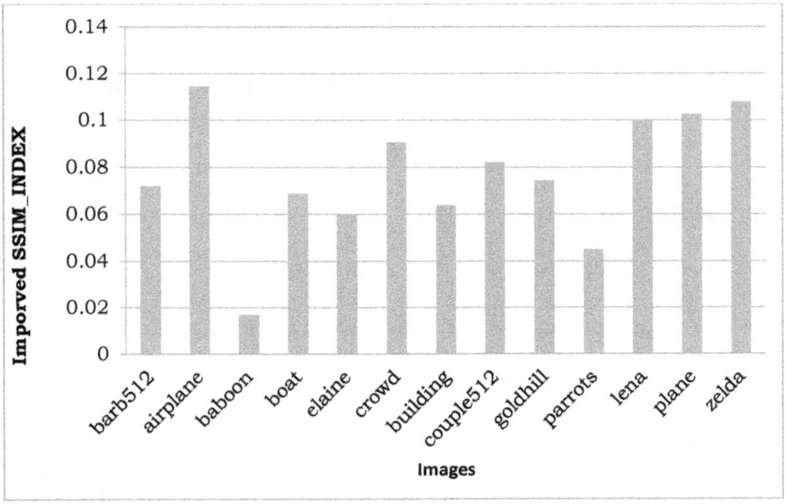

Fig 4.12: Improved SSIM_INDEX when compared to S.gujjunoori et.al., scheme.

From figure 4.11 and 4.12 it is observed that there is an improvement in SSIM_INDEX when compared to the S.gujjunoori et.al scheme (blue).

4.7 SUMMARY

When non-zero coefficients are considered then for an image there is degradation in visual quality which arises in the embedding process when ambiguity is eliminated. When the ambiguity is eliminated the visual quality is improved by minimizing the use of non-zero coefficients, in middle frequency coefficients the data is embedded by the proposed scheme RDH_AVQ. In terms of SSIM_INDEX, SSIM and PSNR, the image visual quality can be improved. For military communication, remote sensing, etc., this scheme can be used and which focuses on reversibility and visual quality.

Chapter - 5

POLYNOMIAL BASED NEAR REVERSIBLE DATA HIDING SCHEME USING DCT (NRDH_POLY)

5.1 INTRODUCTION

For better understanding of what a digital image is, the primary thing is to recognize what we see actually when a "digital image" is placed. Within the computer the digital image itself is really a data structure, and in the image for each pixel or picture element a number or code is contained by it. The color of that pixel is determined by this code. As a discrete sample of a continuous real image the each pixel can be thought. We have to think in many common ways a digital image is created and it is useful. A digital camera, a paint or drawing package, a 3D rendering program, or a page or slide scanner from these a digital image can be created. The digital image can be better understood by the digital camera. With the help of digital camera a digital image is shown in figure 5.1. Here in this example to a scene in the world the camera is aimed, and by the lens onto the camera's picture plane the light is focused from the scene. In a grid-like array the camera's picture plane contains photo sensors are arranged and in the resulting image we can see one sensor for each pixel. To the intensity of the light falling on it the voltage is proportional which is emitted by each sensor, and the for the purpose of storage in a cell of computer memory to the binary or number code the voltage is converted by an analog to digital conversion circuit and the pixel's value is the binary code. A 2D array of pixel values is the typical storage structure, they are arranged such that in memory with row and column numbers the layout of pixel values is organized into a regular grid and corresponding with the row and column numbers of the photo sensor who are reading this pixel's value. Since a finite area is contained by each photo sensor, as indicated by the circles in Figure 5.1

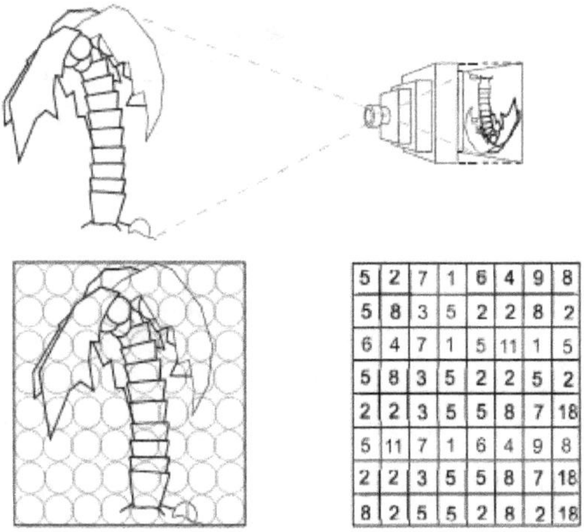

5	2	7	1	6	4	9	8
5	8	3	5	2	2	8	2
6	4	7	1	5	11	1	5
5	8	3	5	2	2	5	2
2	2	3	5	5	8	7	18
5	11	7	1	6	4	9	8
2	2	3	5	5	8	7	18
8	2	5	5	2	8	2	18

Fig 5.1: Capturing a 2D Continuous Image of a Scene

The light falling over its surface for this the weighted average is noted by the reading. So, although each pixel is conceptually the spread of light which centered at the sample point over a small area is represented by the sample of a single point on the camera's image plane. Over the area of the sample to describe how the weighted average is obtained from the weighting function is used called a point spread function. The photoelectric properties of the photo sensor surface focus of the camera and the complex combination of photo sensor size and shape is the exact form of the point spread function. In Figure 5.2 the diagram is form is encountered in a digital camera by sampling through a point spread function of a shape.

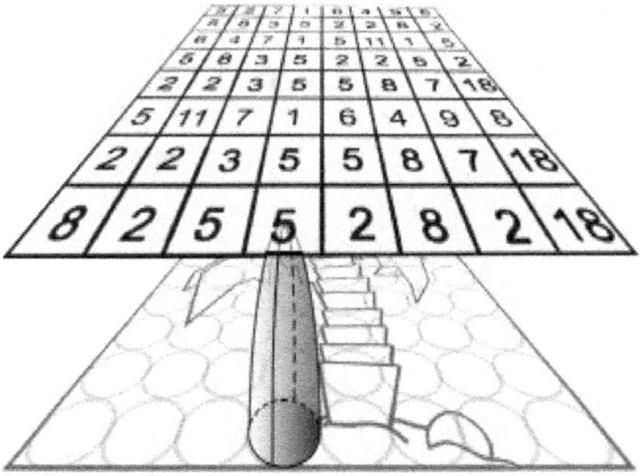

Fig 5.2: Sampling Through a Point-Spread Function

If the digital image cannot be viewed it is of little use. To invert the sampling process there must be as reconstruction process so that from a real continuous scene the discretely sampled image may be recreated. As a continuous image the discrete image samples must be converted by this process which is suitable for output on a device like a CRT or LCD for viewing, or a printer or film recorder for hardcopy. Through the notion of the point spread function this process can also be understood. Think of each sample (i.e. pixel) being passed back Through a point spread function in the digital image the each sample is being passed back that spreads the pixel value out over a small region.

5.2 REPRESENTATION OF DIGITAL IMAGES

A discrete signal having two-dimensional (2D) is a digital image. As a function of two independent variables the signals can be represented mathematically - for examples, a brightness function of two spatial variables. As a 2D array of luminance values a digital image I(x,y) of monochrome type can be defined. A group of pixles is an image. In m*n matrix form the image is representation as

$$I(x,y) = \begin{pmatrix} I(0,0),\ I\ (0,1), \ldots\ldots\ldots\ldots\ldots\ldots\ldots\ldots I(0,n-1) \\ I(1,0),\ I\ (1,1), \ldots\ldots\ldots\ldots\ldots\ldots\ldots\ldots I(1,n-1) \\ \ldots\ldots\ldots\ldots\ldots, \ldots\ldots\ldots\ldots\ldots\ldots\ldots\ldots \\ I(m-1,\ 0),\ I(0,1), \ldots\ldots\ldots\ldots\ldots\ldots I(m-1,n-1) \end{pmatrix}$$

where the intensity (L) of the pixel (i,j) is deonted by I(i,j) and 0<= I(x,y) <=L and L=255.

In various formats the images are classified and there are given below:

Grey scale images: In the form of rectangle one represent a gray scale image, from black to white in the continuous range the luminance is contained by every point in the image. In a computer for the purpose of storing an image for finite precision representation the image need to be discrete and quantized.

Color Images: By three matrices the color images can be represented. To represent the primary color component one of the matrix is used and the Red(R), green (G) and blue (B) are primary colors. Most of the visible colors are represented with the help of these primary colors. Than to color differences to the luminance differences the human eye is much more sensitive.

Luminance Matrix Y: this is the image luminance, and for three primary color components these are the weighted mean.

Chrominance Matrix U: the difference in red is given by this i.e, the luminance and red color component difference.

Chrominance Matrix V: the difference in blue is given by this i.e., the luminance and blue color component difference.

In the process of analog image to digital image conversion between the three different ways one color need to be chosen for representing an image.

24-bit color: The 224 colors are displayed at a time per pixel, and as different quantities like: red(R), green (G) and blue (B) these can be represented.

8-bit color: The 256 (2^8) colors are displayed at a time per pixel and as a table of colors or from a palette they are chosen.

8-bit grey-scale: This provides 256 (2^8) shades of grey per pixel.

Pixels and Bitmaps

With pixels the digital images are made (short for picture elements). In image at a single point the color is represented by each pixel, so as a tiny dot of a particular color the pixel looks like. The digital approximation of the image is created when at a points of large number the color of an image is measured. In the form of rows and columns they are arranged in a conventional photographic image and they seems to be like grain particles and in distinct way the information is stored. The digital image can be described as a rectangular form of arrays.

5.2.1 Types of Digital Images

Images are of two types 1) color image 2) black and white images. With the colored pixels the color images are formed while the black and white images are made in different shades of gray with the help of pixels.

Black and White Images

With the help of pixels the images of black and white are formed and at a particular location the pixel holding a single value corresponds to the image's gray level. In a series of very fine steps from black to white normally 256 different grays levels these gray levels in the full range. Since about 200 different gray levels the eye can rarely distinguish.

It is assumed that there are 256 gray levels and storage process for each pixel of black and white is stored in one byte of memory.

Color Images

With the help of pixels a color image is made and where at a particular location each pixel had three numbers which corresponds to the red, green, and blue levels of the image. The additive primary colors are those which are used for mixing light and those colors are red, green, and blue when compared with primary colors there is a difference in subtractive primary colors and for mixing paints these subtractive colors are used. By mixing these primary colors in a proper proportion any color can be obtained. It is assumed that for each primary color there are 256 levels and for the purpose of storing each pixel the requirement of memory is three bytes (24 bits). The different colors that are possible are 16.7 million colors.

5.2.2 Color Terminology

According to the levels of red, green, and blue the pixels are stored in the computer; with this method the specification of colors is different from we normally recognize the colors. To specify colors there are many unique ways, the effective way of specifying is to separate out the brightness components of a color, saturation, and hue.

When other colors are mixed there is no possibility of getting the Primary colors. Using three different sets of wavelengths we can recognize the colors by using three primary colors. When these three primary colors are mixed any color can be represented. In two distinct ways these colors can be combined additive and subtractive color mixing.

Most of us during school days learned about subtractive color mixing and on a piece of paper how the two colored paints or inks can be combined is described by it. The Cyan, Magenta, and Yellow are the three subtractive primaries. When two different colors of lights are combined is called Additive color mixing, for example on the same white wall when two colored spotlights are shined. In computer at different proportions when the combination process of red, green, and blue light beams are completed then on the face of the monitor an image is displayed and formed. The subtractive color model are used by color printers. A fourth color is used so that the impure nature of most printing inks can be compensated, since by combining cyan, magenta the black is obtained rather than a deep rich black and by using a murky dark green yellow inks is often obtained. Because of the above circumstances in magazines a 4-color process is used so that color images are produced by a commercial color printing presses. A secondary color is obtained when in equal amounts the two primary colors are mixed.

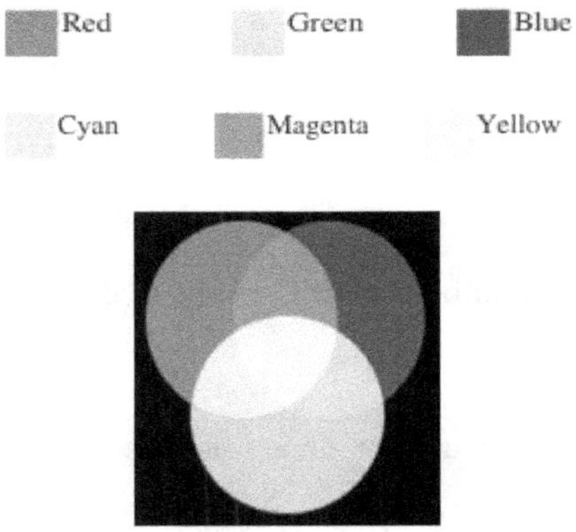

5.2.3 Color Gamut

When the three primary colors are blended one cannot obtain the any visible color. On paper or computer screens the colors are obtained with the help of the dyes, pigments, and phosphors and the colors obtained are imperfect and by them the visible colors full range cannot be recreated. The color gamut is a particular device or medium by which the actual range of colors can be achievable and to some extent but not completely and by the characteristics of its primary colors this is determined. The different color gamuts are present in photographic film, scanners, computer monitors and printers and the quite challenging problem is to achieve consistent color. Because of total dynamic range the different media may differ.

■Red ■Green ■Blue

■Cyan ■Magenta ■Yellow

Color Management

The definition of color management is the process of acquiring an image and this image when it is in two or more different media or devices it has to look the same, and in today's world we can see the availability of different color management systems. But tactlessly maximum of them are complex, expensive, and these are not suitable/unavailable for a full range of devices.

Hue

It identifies what a color or a shade is present. For instance, the hue value is similar for all reds irrespective of their intense, or pastel.

Saturation

In what quantity the colors intensity and purity can be identified or measured by the saturation of a color. To identify how a saturated color looks like is that the color should be deep and brilliant— the color gets lighter and it seems to be washed out because of the decrement in saturation.

Brightness

To know whether the color is light or dark it is identified by the brightness of a color. The color is black if it's brightness is made to zero, nonetheless of its hue or saturation. A color's brightness is specified by different schemes and there is variation in brightness when lightening of a color takes place depending on which one is used.

Luminance

From a given direction from a surface per unit area the amount of intensity of light emitted is called luminance. The fact that to certain colors (like yellow-green) the eye of human is sensitive than to others (like blue) which is taken into account by computation of luminance.

Chrominance

To luminance the complementary concept is a Chrominance. There are two components to determine how a television signal works—the chrominance information contained by luminance and a color signal and is represented by black and white image. A 2-dimensional color space is Chrominance where the hue and saturation are represented independent of brightness.

5.3 SAGAR et. al., SCHEME

As input the reference image is taken in Sagar et.al., system and the reference image is divided in to 8×8 blocks of intensity values it is portioned and on each block a 2-dimensional DCT is applied. With the help of 8×8 block quantization table the each block is divided. In embedding process, Sagar et. al.,. scheme [75] which used logarithmic function. This scheme achieves reversibility and high capacity, lags good visual quality which has to be addressed. For embedding Sagar et.al., scheme considers all the nonzero AC coefficients. Because of this low PSNR is achieved, it strikes less visual quality [57, 69].

5.4 NRDH_POLY SCHEME

The visual quality, robustness and hiding capacity are essential features of any scheme of data hiding. Depending on user's requirements and applications domains to each application the changes among three features vary specifically. For applications like copyright protection of remote sensing images [37] there is a need of scheme called data hiding (near reversible). But in this the entire focus is on the visual quality, there by proposing the polynomial based near reversible scheme using DCT it can be done. To achieve this objective i.e., in terms of PSNR [9] the visual quality need to be improved. We are ignoring the low frequency i.e., non-zero coefficients of DCT to improve the PSNR values. As a result, there is reduction in embedding capacity and NK is almost same but achieving the good visual quality in the form of PSNR. When the multimedia content is not clear instead of considering low frequency we go for middle and high frequency of the multimedia content. When low frequency component are altered we can see poor visual quality. As in the Figure 5.3 Zig-Zag scan process is used so that the visual quality is increased. The scan List of Zig-Zag we are considering from the quantized DCT values from i=11

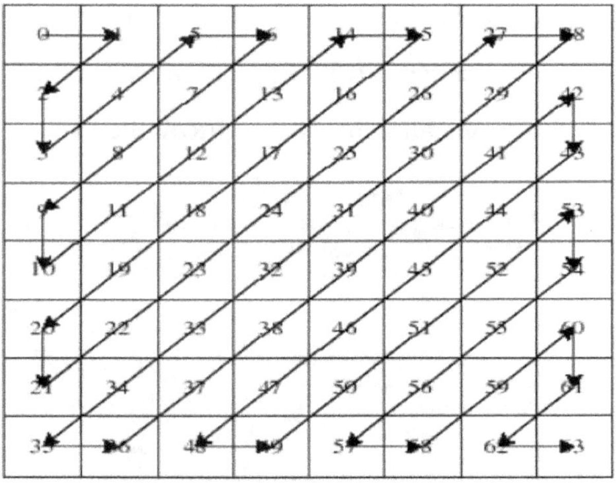

Fig 5.3: Zig-Zag Scan Process

Zig-Zag scanning is move from low to high frequency component of 8 × 8 block. In low frequency most of the energy stored. The scan is favored and applied to a non uniform quantization of N X N DCT [46] coefficients before run length coding. Advantage of this structure the Zig- Zag scans instructs the coefficients of DCT are efficient for this coding phase. This scanning is quite optimal for lossless compression tasks. After a zigzag ordering DCT compression completes. A polynomial based mathematical function is used to achieve the above objective i.e., improvement in visual quality. As input the input image is taken and in to 8 × 8 blocks of intensity there is a partition of input image and on each block a 2- dimensional DCT is implemented. By quantization table of 8 × 8 block the each block is divided. For each block Zig-Zag scan algorithm and in Zig-Zag scanned list we have to consider the quantized DCT values from i=11. In embedding process, there is embedment of data in all non-zero DCT coefficients i.e. as shown in Figure 5.4 in that block the data is embedded only when the block having non-zero DCT coefficient number greater than zero.

5.4.1 Data embedding process of NRDH_POLY

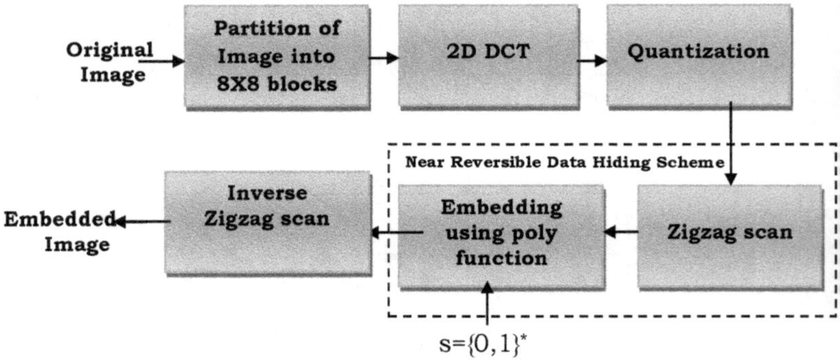

Fig 5.4: Embedding process of NRDH_POLY

In each block except the blocks equal to zero, in all non-zero DCT Coefficients pixels the data is embedded. The design is NRDH_POLY to for better visual quality by reducing the modifications in the original coefficients i.e. to nearer value of original coefficients the watermarked coefficients are retained. Polynomial function is used to transform the generated DCT coefficients for hiding the secret data.

5.4.2 Embedding Algorithm with example of NRDH_POLY

As an input the embedding algorithm takes the 512 x 512 gray scale images. Then on each image by applying DCT followed by quantization the quantized coefficient is calculated. Then, by using the zigzag scan in quantized coefficients the secret data will be embedded.

Example : As shown in table 5.1 an 8 x 8 portion of cover image (lena image) is considered and the embedded algorithm is applied.

Solution: for input 8 x 8 matrices first generate the DCT matrix. Then apply quantization on 8 x 8 matrix, like this apply all sub images of 512 x 512 gray scale image. After quantization into quantized coefficients the secret data is embedded. To select the quantized coefficients zigzag scan is used. Then, de-quantization is performed and on embedded coefficients inverse DCT is performed. The stego-object pixels is generated by this process. the input table of 8x8 block as shown in table 5.1.

Table 5.1: Input 8x8 matrix

159	155	140	146	148	159	164	159
157	157	148	155	162	164	159	157
159	150	157	159	157	157	157	162
157	159	159	164	157	157	159	157
155	159	162	159	155	159	159	157
162	159	157	155	159	162	155	155
164	162	159	162	159	159	159	155
159	157	162	159	159	157	157	157

From each entry as shown in table 5.2 by subtracting 128 the original block is "levelled off" so that for pixel values ranging from -128 to 127 the DCT is designed.

Table 5.2: leveled off 8x8 block

31	27	12	18	20	31	36	31
29	29	20	27	34	36	31	29
31	22	29	31	29	29	29	34
29	31	31	36	29	29	31	29
27	31	34	31	27	31	31	29
34	31	29	27	31	34	27	27
36	34	31	34	31	31	31	27
31	29	34	31	31	29	29	29

The resultant 8x8 matrix, after applying DCT on 8x8 matrix coefficients are shown in table 5.3.

Table 5.3: 8x8 block after DCT

237.37	-2.20	3.22	7.19	0.12	2.59	-0.38	-3.40
-9.80	-12.62	8.14	7.17	1.33	-0.33	-3.45	-3.62
-4.96	-3.68	7.57	8.60	0.46	-1.27	-2.829	-0.17
-4.10	-0.25	7.11	7.82	-5.59	-2.37	-2.40	-2.78
-3.62	-1.58	2.91	-5.22	-4.37	2.55	-2.42	-0.59
0.21	2.30	4.28	-0.67	1.64	4.27	-2.73	-1.83
-5.11	-1.99	4.42	-0.56	2.10	0.81	4.92	2.20
-0.88	-1.42	2.60	-4.07	-0.21	3.15	1.68	1.02

Resultant quantized DCT coefficients 8x8 matrix, after quantization on DCT coefficients is shown in table 5.4

Table 5.4: 8x8 block of DCT Quantized

15	0	0	0	0	0	0	0
-1	-1	1	0	0	0	0	0
0	0	0	1	0	0	0	0
0	0	0	0	0	0	0	0
0	0	0	0	0	0	0	0
0	0	0	0	0	0	0	0
0	0	0	0	0	0	0	0
0	0	0	0	0	0	0	0

Resultant embedded matrix, after embedding secret data on quantized coefficients of 8 x 8 block shown in table 5.5

Table 5.5: 8x8 block

15	0	0	0	0	0	0	0
-1	-1	1	0	0	0	0	0
0	0	0	2	0	0	0	0
0	0	0	0	0	0	0	0
0	0	0	0	0	0	0	0
0	0	0	0	0	0	0	0
0	0	0	0	0	0	0	0
0	0	0	0	0	0	0	0

On embedded 8 x 8 blocks as shown in table 5.6 the de-quantization and inverse DCT is applied.

Table 5.6: stego 8x8 block

163	**153**	**145**	**148**	**158**	**164**	**161**	**155**
159	**155**	**151**	**151**	**156**	**160**	**160**	**159**
154	**157**	**158**	**157**	**154**	**154**	**158**	**163**
151	**159**	**165**	**161**	**153**	**150**	**157**	**165**
152	**160**	**167**	**164**	**155**	**151**	**156**	**164**
156	**160**	**164**	**163**	**159**	**156**	**156**	**158**
162	**160**	**159**	**161**	**164**	**163**	**157**	**152**
166	**160**	**155**	**159**	**167**	**167**	**158**	**147**

From the table 5.1 and table 5.6 the no of bits is embedded based on zigzag scan and the scan started position. So, it can conclude that distortion is more or less same as Sagar et.al., scheme by embedding secret data using NRDH_POLY embedding algorithm, but against compression it is strong enough. And also, the quantization in embedding process purely depends on cover content.

Algorithm: Embedding Algorithm of NRDH_POLY

Step 1. Take an input image I and

Step 2. Partition I using DCT I→ $\{B_{1,}B_2, \ldots . B_l\}$

For each $B_j \in I$, where $1 \leq j \leq 8$

(a) In $B_j$as below the DCT coefficients are quantized.

for $i_1 \leftarrow 1$ to 8 do

for $i_2 \leftarrow 1$ to 8 do

$C_j(i_1, i_2) = B_j(i_1, i_2)/Q(i_1, i_2)$;

end

end

Step 3. Zig-Zag scan applied

(a) Compute T as shown in function (1) after converting the matrix to row or column vectorization, if $T > 0$, there is a modification in all the AC non-zero coefficients and using function (2) the data is embedded. Let the resultant block be C_j.

Step 4. Inverse Zig-Zag Scan is applied

Step 5. Combine all the $C_j$blocks into I= $\{C_{1,}C_2, \ldots . C_l\}$.

Step 6. For all the blocks repeat step 1 to step 5.

$$T = \sum_{j=11}^{64} C_j \qquad (1)$$

$$E = \begin{cases} \sqrt{(6c^2 - 4c + 7) * 0.47\ if\ S = 0} \\ \sqrt{(6c^2 - 4c + 7) * 0.5\ if\ S = 1} \end{cases} \qquad (2)$$

Where is the non-zero DCT Coefficient, the secret bit be Sand Em be the modified version of c.

5.4.3 Data Extraction Process of NRDH_POLY

The extraction procedure extracts the image with rounded values of the real part of the polynomial functions (4) are used to restore [18] the generated DCT coefficients when the Secret bit S=0 or 1.

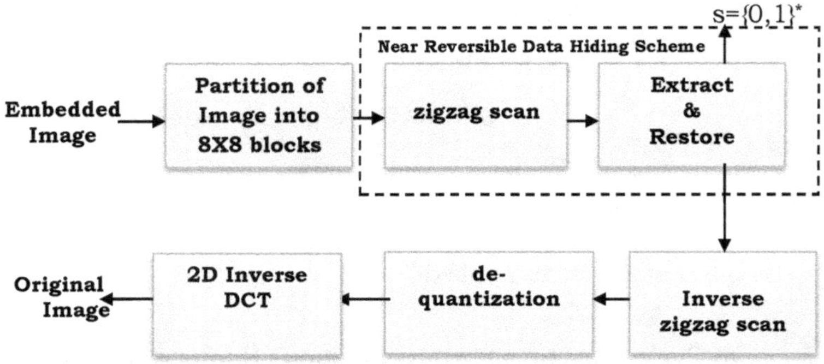

Fig 5.5: Extraction process of NRDH_POLY

5.4.4 Extraction Algorithm with example of NRDH_POLY

1. Take an watermarked input image (*I*)
2. Extract C_j from I.← $\{C_1, C_2, \ldots . C_l\}$
3. *Zig-Zag is Applied*

   for each $C_j \in I$

   (a) when T > 0

   i. Using (3) the data bits are extracted.

   ii. Using (4) the modified coefficients are restored.

   Let the resultant block be E_j

4. Inverse Zig-Zag is Applied
5. In the following way the E_j elements are dequantized:

   for $i_1 \leftarrow 1$ to 8 do

   for $i_2 \leftarrow 1$ to 8 do

   $$R_j(i_1, i_2) = E_j(i_1, i_2) \times Q(i_1, i_2);$$

   end

   end

   R_j= IDCT(R_j);

   end

To get *I i.e.* $I = \{R_1, R_2, \ldots, R_l\}$ all the blocks R_j are combined.

6. for all embedded $R_j \in I$, repeat step 1 to step 5.

$$I_j = \begin{cases} 0 & \text{if e\%2} = 0, \\ 1 & \text{otherwise.} \end{cases} \quad (3)$$

$$E_x = \begin{cases} \left(\left({}^{c}/_{0.47}\right)^2\right) - 7 \; if \; s = 0 \\ \left(\left({}^{c}/_{0.47}\right)^2\right) - 7 \; if \; s = 1 \end{cases} \quad (4)$$

E_x is the restored version of original c.

Communication that the embedding and extraction procedure is near-reversible. The extraction algorithm takes input as 512 x 512 stego grayscale image. Then apply de-quantization on the quantized coefficients followed by applying Inverse DCT and combine all blocks of 8 x 8 to get the original cover content.

Example: As shown in table 5.6 8x8 block of a stego object (Arieal12 image) is taken and the extraction algorithm is applied.

Answer: To the all blocks of image first apply DCT transform and quantization for input 8x8 block. Then extract the secret data form quantized coefficients. Then, on extracted blocks of 8x8 matrices the de-quantization and the inverse DCT is performed.

Table 5.7: stego 8x8 block

163	153	145	148	158	164	161	155
159	155	151	151	156	160	160	159
154	157	158	157	154	154	158	163
151	159	165	161	153	150	157	165
152	160	167	164	155	151	156	164
156	160	164	163	159	156	156	158
162	160	159	161	164	163	157	152
166	160	155	159	167	167	158	147

Resultant blocks, after the de-quantization applied the table is shown in 5.7

Table 5.8: De-Quantization 8x8 block

480	0	0	0	0	0	0	0
12	0	0	0	0	0	0	0
0	0	0	0	0	0	0	0
0	0	0	0	0	0	0	0
0	0	0	0	0	0	0	0
0	0	0	0	0	0	0	0
0	0	0	0	0	0	0	0
0	0	0	0	0	0	0	0

Inverse DCT is applied on input 8x8 block is shown in 5.8

Table 5.9: IDCT 8x8 block

34.73	25.25	17.26	19.81	29.68	35.94	33.21	27.44
31.18	26.64	22.54	23.25	27.84	31.69	32.05	30.66
26.27	28.81	30.34	28.50	25.54	25.81	30.31	34.95
23.11	30.89	36.70	33.20	24.70	21.94	28.80	37.32
23.82	32.17	38.70	35.5	26.56	22.64	28.13	35.73
28.31	32.45	36.03	35.10	30.84	27.80	28.41	30.45
34.22	32.08	31.07	33.13	35.77	34.68	29.21	23.92
38.32	31.68	27.32	31.46	39.04	39.46	29.85	19.49

By appling the de-quantization and inverse DCT on embedded matrix shown in 5.9. After extraction the resultant 8X8 block is obtained as shown in 5.10.

Table 5.10: After extraction 8x8 block

163	153	145	148	158	164	161
159	155	151	151	156	160	160
154	157	158	157	154	154	158
151	159	165	161	153	150	157
152	160	167	164	155	151	156
156	160	164	163	159	156	156
162	160	159	161	164	163	157
166	160	155	159	167	167	158

5.5 RESULTS AND ANALYSIS

Using MATLAB, the NRDH_POLY scheme is implemented. We used GIF 512 X 512 formatted grayscale images in the implementation.

Table 5.11: Sagar et.al., and NRDH_POLY function behaviors

values	Non-zero DCT coefficients Values	Selected NRDH_POLY Function2	NRDH_POLY Function3	Sagar et.al., Function4	Selected NRDH_POLY Function5	NRDH_POLY Function6
1	1	2	2	2	1	2
2	2	2	3	4	2	3
3	3	4	5	5	3	4
4	4	5	7	6	4	6
5	5	6	8	6	6	7
6	6	7	10	7	7	8
7	7	8	12	7	8	10
8	8	9	13	8	9	11
9	9	11	15	8	10	13
10	10	12	17	8	11	14
11	11	12	18	8	12	16
12	12	14	20	9	13	17
13	13	16	22	9	15	19
14	14	17	23	9	16	20
15	15	18	25	9	17	22
16	16	19	27	10	18	23
17	17	20	29	10	19	25
18	18	22	30	10	20	24
19	19	23	32	10	22	27
20	20	24	34	10	23	29
21	21	25	35	10	24	30
22	22	27	37	10	25	32
23	23	28	39	11	26	33
24	24	29	41	11	27	35
25	25	30	42	11	28	36

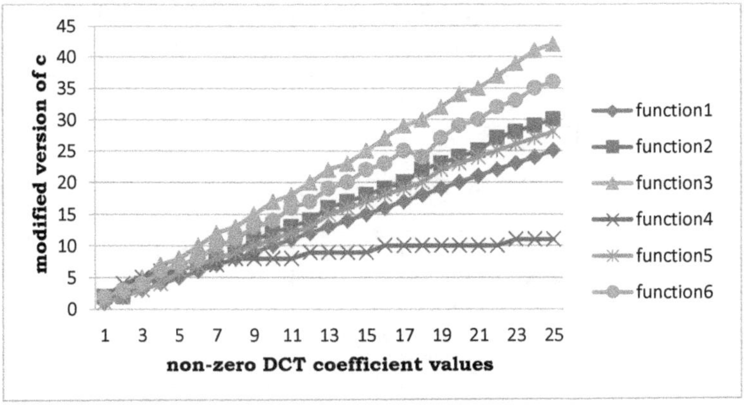

Fig 5.6: Behavior of Sagar et.al., function and NRDH_POLY functions

Where function 1 is y=AC coefficients of original image,

Function 2 is $\sqrt{(6c^2 - 4c + 7)} * 0.5$

Function 3 is $\sqrt{(6c^2 - 4c + 7)} * 0.7$

Function 4 is. $y = \lfloor 2\, log_2(2|c|) \rfloor$

Function 5 is $\sqrt{(6c^2 - 4c + 7)} * 0.47$

Function 6 is $\sqrt{(6c^2 - 4c + 7)} * 0.6$

Where the non-zero DCT coefficient is 'c' and y be is the modified version of c. From the graph, we can observe that function 4 changes drastically with respect to their original coefficients which cause the distortion or unclear. From function 2 and function 5 graphs it is observed that because they retain maximum values to original values. Here we have chosen function 2 and 5 for hiding the data from table 5.11 & figure 5.6.

Table 5.12: embedded capacity of Sagar et.al., and NRDH_POLY scheme

	Embedded Capacity	
Image	**Sagar et.al., Scheme**	**NRDH_POLY Scheme**
Aerial	56562	28652
Airplane	12608	4318
Baboon	74002	44542
Barb	39346	18651
Boat	36279	14437
Couple	34360	13829
Elaine	27556	8117
Goldhill	38190	14613
Lena	30767	13475
Truck	33618	13107

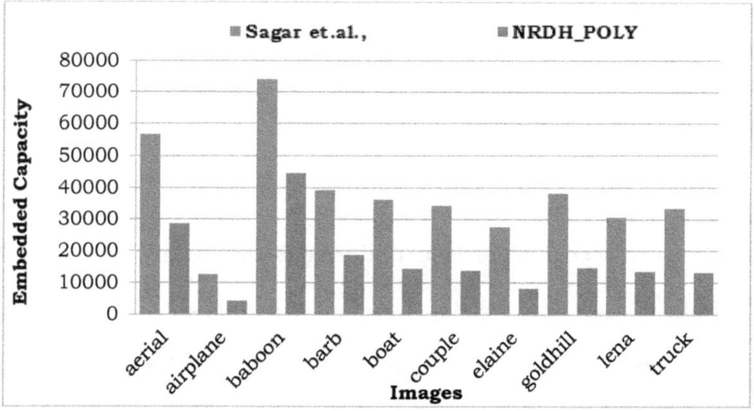

Fig 5.7: Comparison of Capacity

We can observe from the table 5.12 & figure 5.7 that Sagar et.al., scheme and NRDH_POLY scheme results are not same because we are ignoring the low frequency non-zero coefficients so that there is improvement in visual quality, there is reduction in embedding capacity.

Table 5.13: Normal correlation of Sagar et.al., and NRDH_POLY scheme

Images	Normal Correlation	
	Sagar et.al., Scheme	**NRDH_POLY Scheme**
Aerial	0.998	0.9943
Airplane	0.9997	0.9994
Baboon	0.9979	0.9786
Barb	0.9982	0.9854
Boat	0.9983	0.996
Couple	0.9977	0.9922
Elaine	0.9991	0.9991
Goldhill	0.9988	0.9966
Lena	0.9975	0.9949
Truck	0.9979	0.9976

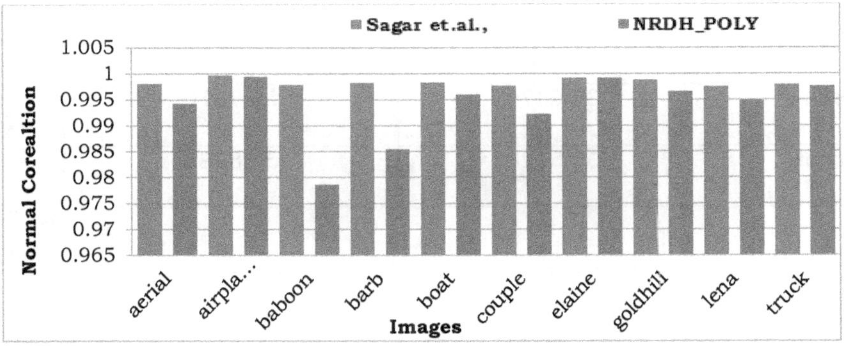

Fig 5.8: Comparison of NK

As the Normalized Cross-Correlation checks the identity between images where [0, 1] and more the value near to one the more they are highly correlated, we can achieve them from table 5.13 & figure 5.8 that the

NRDH_POLY scheme achieve values more nearer to one than the Sagar et.al., scheme. Hence, NRDH_POLY scheme is highly correlated and achieves almost same NK than the Sagar et.al., scheme.

Table 5.14: visual quality of Sagar et.al., and NRDH_POLY scheme

	PSNR	
Images	**Sagar et.al., Scheme**	**NRDH_POLY Scheme**
Aerial	32.141	48.1465
Airplane	40.7976	57.8019
Baboon	33.469	46.1276
Barb	34.9173	49.7633
Boat	34.9788	52.3637
Couple	35.0741	51.8653
Elaine	37.8969	56.7113
Goldhill	37.2432	53.5468
Lena	35.2476	52.7576
Truck	35.5128	54.8288

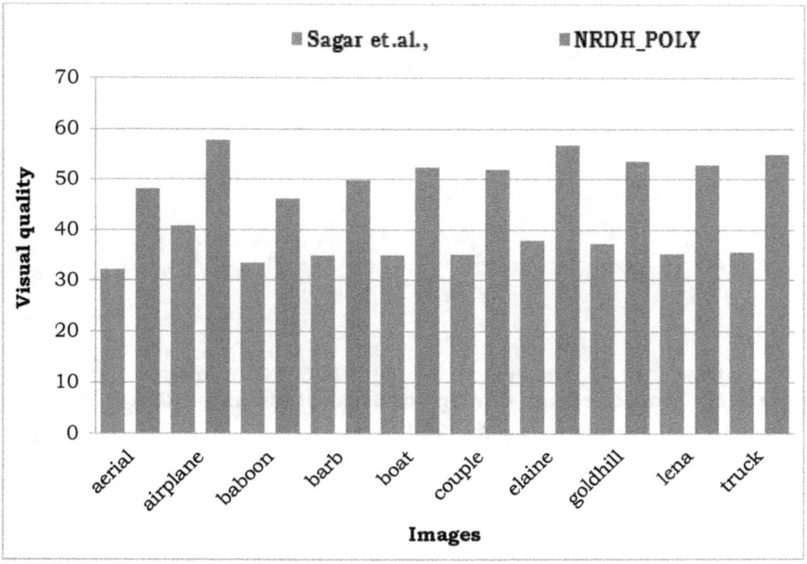

Fig 5.9: Comparison of PSNR

Than Sagar et.al., scheme the better PSNR is achieved by the NRDH_POLY scheme and it can be observed from the table 5.14 & figure 5.9.

Therefore, than the Sagar et.al., scheme NRDH_POLY scheme performs better because ignoring the low frequency non-zero coefficients of DCT. We present different images of GIF format (fig 5.10 to fig 5.17) of size in the following and their corresponding distorted images can also be observed from all observations, we can find that the Sagar et.al., scheme distorts the images more where as the NRDH_POLY scheme achieves better visual quality.

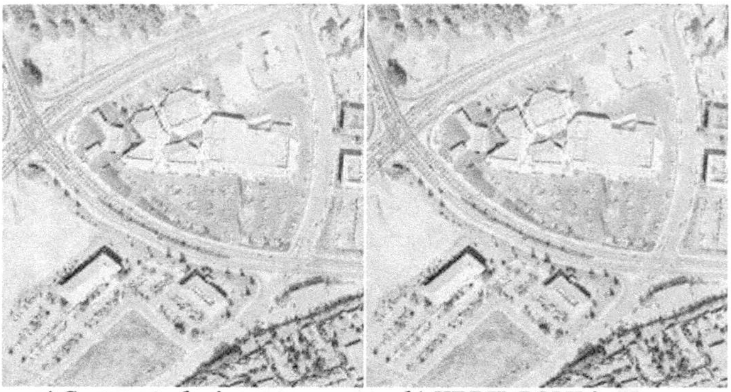

a) Sagar et.al., image b) NRDH_POLY image

Figure 5.10: Embedded aerial image of Sagar et.al., and NRDH_POLY scheme

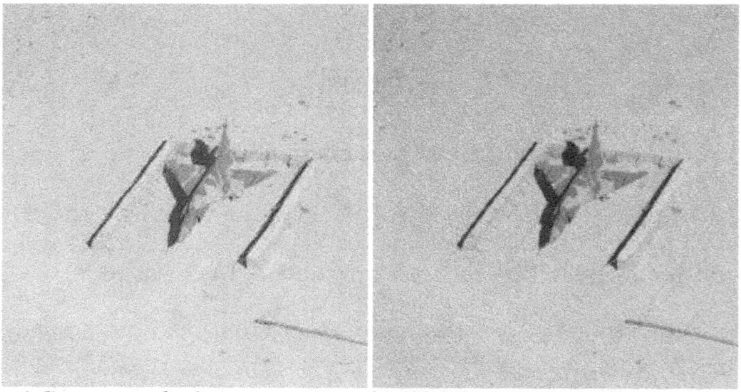

a) Sagar et.al., image b) NRDH_POLY image

Fig 5.11: Embedded aircraft image of Sagar et.al., and NRDH_POLY scheme

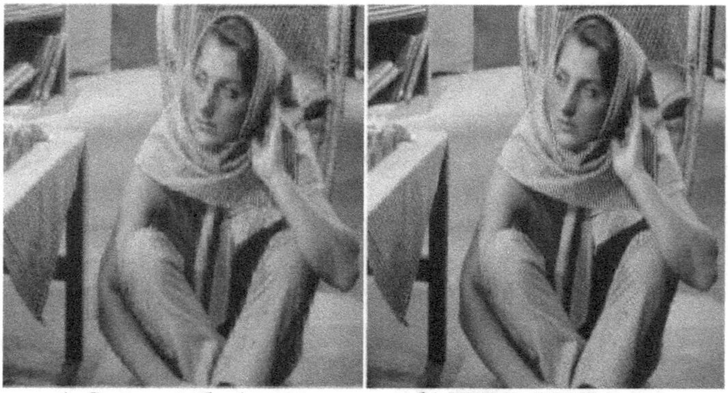

a) Sagar et.al., image b) NRDH_POLY image

Fig 5.12: Embedded Barb image of Sagar et.al., & NRDH_POLY scheme

a) Sagar et.al., image b) NRDH_POLY image:

Fig 5.13: Embedded boat image of Sagar et.al., and NRDH_POLY scheme

a) Sagar et.al., image b) NRDH_POLY image

Fig 5.14: Embedded Couple image of Sagar et.al., & NRDH_POLY Scheme

a) Sagar et.al., image b) NRDH_POLY image

Fig 5.15: Embedded Elaine image of Sagar et.al., and NRDH_POLY scheme

a) Sagar et.al., image b) NRDH_POLY image

Fig 5.16: Embedded Lena image of Sagar et.al., & NRDH_POLY scheme

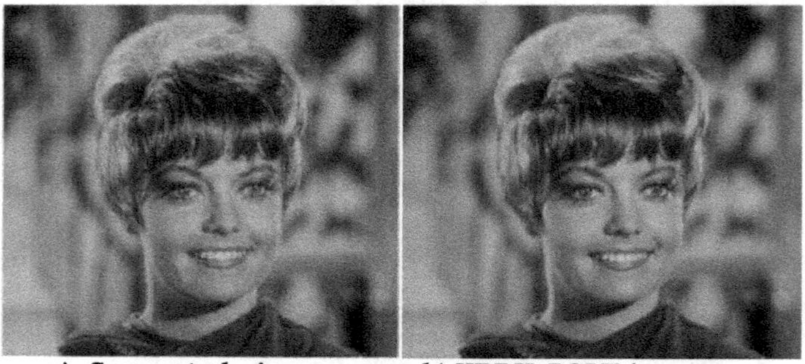

a) Sagar et.al., image b) NRDH_POLY image

Fig 5.17: Embedded Zelda image of Sagar et.al., & NRDH_POLY scheme

5.6 SUMMARY

The growth of new type near reversible data embedding, there is a need for more refined scheme. The near reversible scheme addressed many applications of remote sensing. The visual quality degrades and generates many unclear images because, use of log function which transforms the coefficients with greater difference. The proposed scheme achieves higher visual quality as it minimizes the difference between original non-zero DCT coefficients to the embedded coefficients.

Chapter - 6

HVS BASED NEAR REVERSIBLE DATA EMBEDDING (NRDH_MATH)

6.1 INTRODUCTION

The visual evaluation of Digital data is the primary task of many image and video processing tools. Two types of Image Quality Assessment metrics [45,2] are present 1) subjective 2) objective both are used for evaluation. The subjective evaluation is done by viewers. By using assessment metrics the objective evaluation is done. The subjective evaluation assessment uses more number of human viewers are involved in subjective evaluation for assessment and it is an expensive as there is involvement of more number of users it becomes complex and more time consuming. Consequently, Peak Signal-to-Noise Ratio (PSNR) is considered, which is a objective model and with viewer's opinion it basically does not correlate well. Many metrics are developed after wide research in this area on Human Visual System (HVS), these are basic metrics.

The P_HVS, MSSIM and P_HVS_M are the metrics used which are based on HVS. P_HVS and by taking the Human Visual System (HVS) the calculation of Peak signal to noise ratio (PSNR) metric is completed. The difference between the coefficients contrast masking of DCT basis function and contrast sensitivity function (CSF) is calculated by the metric P_HVS_M based on HVS. Between two images the similarity is found out by Index metric using Structural Similarity (SSIM) where one image should be of ideal quality. For the purposing of addressing the limitations like more alterations to the coefficients or pixels the extended research area has been upward. The more challenging trade-off is the triangular trade-off between visual quality capacities, robustness. There is a call for Near Reversible Data Hiding scheme which is HVS based to accomplish better visual quality. In remote sensing such as tsunami, volcanic eruption that is the natural disasters it has emerged applications etc., it captures the image. In Reversible Data Hiding shows the facts of low embedding capacity and complexity. Already exist a few Near Reversible Hiding schemes deals with capacity, robustness and visual quality metrics. There is a warning to the multimedia content owners because of growth in technology. Because of this improvement forward image, audio and video are easily and illegally forwarded to users. To design any scheme the hidden data can be secret information to cover content. Some schemes are Near Reversible schemes for applications like copyright protection these are useful.

6.2 HVS BASED VISUAL QUALITY METRICS

For evaluation the metrics we use the Image Quality Assessment (IQA) metrics which are based on subjective and objective. The assessment metrics are considered for objective evaluation.

6.2.1 Peak Signal-To-Noise Ratio (PSNR)

The abbreviation of PSNR is Peak Signal-to-Noise Ratio. For the purpose of indicating the ratio between the possible power of a maximum signal and the corrupting noise power this term is used.

Since a very broad dynamic range is contained by many of signals. In the measurement of PSNR is in logarithmic decibel. For image compression especially in lossy compression codes to measure the restoration quality the PSNR is commonly used. The original data considered as signal in this case and by compression the error is presented which is in the form of noise. To human perception of reconstruction quality it is used as an approximation when comparing compression codes, even though it has a lower PSNR, therefore in some cases to the original data one restoration may appear to be closer than another. Whether the restoration is of higher quality or not represented by a higher PSNR.

While considering the range of this metric validity one has to be particularly careful. To evaluate results from the same content and same codec type it is valid categorically. In equation 6.1 through the Mean Squared Error (MSE) it is defined in a simple manner. Here the two images I and K of order M×N and here as a noisy estimate for the images are considered as:

$$\text{MSE} = \frac{1}{\text{mn}} \sum_{i=0}^{m-1} \sum_{j=0}^{n-1} [I(i,j) - K(i,j)]^2 \tag{6.1}$$

PSNR (in db) is identify in equation 6.2 as

$$\text{PSNR} = 10 log_{10}\left(\frac{MAX_I^2}{MSE}\right) \tag{6.2}$$

The highest probable image pixel value is denoted by MAX_I. More usually, with linear PCM by 8 bits per sample when the examples are represented then MAX_I is 2B−1,.

The three RGB values are used by color images for each pixel, the PSNR definition is identical and MSE is defined as the sum over all squared value differences divided by image size. Alternately, to a different color space the image is converted. In losy image and video compression the distinct values of PSNR is between 30 and 50 dB. Between 20 dB to 25 dB for wireless transmission these are the suitable values. The MSE will be zero when two images are the same. For this value the PSNR is approximate image.

6.2.2 PSNR_HVS

The system taken in to account by the algorithm is Human Visual System, and in figure 6.1 we can see the use of Peak signal-to-noise ratio.

$$P_{HVS} = 10log_{10}\left(\frac{255}{MSE_H}\right) \tag{6.3}$$

In this equation 6.4, MSE_H is considered HVS taking into account .

$$MSE_H = K\sum_{i=1}^{I-7}\sum_{j=1}^{J-7}\sum_{m=1}^{8}\sum_{n=1}^{8}\left(\left(X[m,n]_{ij} - X[m,n]_{ij}^{e}\right)T_c[m,n]\right)^2 \tag{6.4}$$

Where the size of image is given by I & J, and the DCT coefficients of 8×8 block image are given by $k = \frac{1}{[(I-7)(J-7)64]}$ X_{ij} here to the i and j the left upper corner's coordinates are equal, in original image the X_{ij}^{e}

gives the equivalent block of DCT coefficients and the matrix of correcting features is T_c which is taken from the JPEG still picture compression usual as shown in table 6.1 [10].

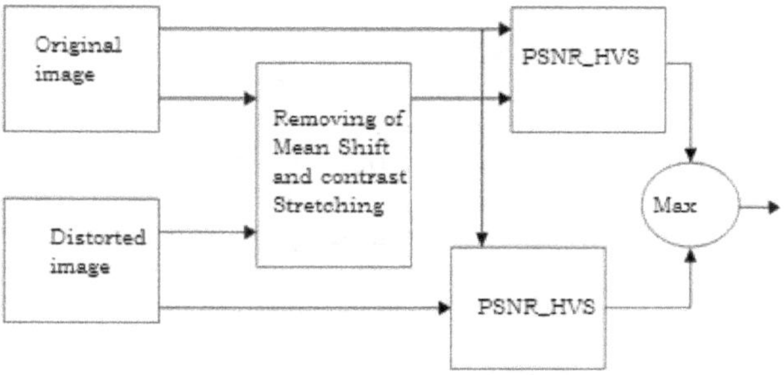

Fig 6.1: Flow-chart of PSNR-HVS calculation

Removing of contrast stretching and mean shifting is achieved using scanning window. The window size of 64×64.

Table 6.1: T_c matrix of correcting factor

1.6084	2.3396	2.5735	1.6084	1.0723	0.6434	0.5046	0.4219
2.1446	2.1446	1.8382	1.3545	0.9898	0.4437	0.4289	0.4679
1.8382	1.9796	1.6084	1.0723	0.6434	0.4515	0.3730	0.4596
1.8382	1.5138	1.1698	0.8874	0.5046	0.2958	0.3217	0.4151
1.4297	1.1698	0.6955	0.4596	0.3785	0.2361	0.2499	0.3342
1.0723	0.7353	0.4679	0.4021	0.3177	0.2475	0.2277	0.2797
0.5252	0.4021	0.3299	0.2958	0.2499	0.2127	0.2145	0.2797
0.3574	0.2797	0.2709	0.2626	0.2298	0.2574	0.2499	0.2600

The following properties of matrix T_c has

The ratio between its coefficients is inversely comparative to ratio of consequent elements in the quantization table of JPEG.

To $\sum_{m=0}^{8}\sum_{n=0}^{8} T_c[m,n]^2/64$ the value of total correcting factor of the matrix is equal to unity. This assures that in case of uniform distribution of distortions between all spatial frequencies the values of MSE_H coincides with MSE.

6.2.3 PSNR_HVS_M

Based on HVS the visual between contrast sensitivity function (CSF) and coefficient contrast masking of DCT basis functions is shown in figure 6.3 by taking PSNR_HVS_M [46] into account. On assumption this metric is dependent and the assumption is that its square value the masking degree of each coefficient X_{ij} depends and to this DCT basis function human eye is sensitivity and by means of CSF it is determined. In an block of 8×8 image block the $E_w(X)$ is the weighted energy of DCT coefficients

$$E_w(X) = \sum_{i=0}^{7}\sum_{j=0}^{7} X_{ij}^2\, C_{ij} \qquad (6.5)$$

Where the DCT coefficient is X_{ij} and i, j are the indices, C_{ij} is the correcting factor and by the CSF it is determined. If

$$E_w(X-Y) < \max\left(E_w(X)/16, E_w(Y)\right)$$

Then the DCT coefficients are distinguished

Where the masking effect C_{ij} of DCT coefficients X is $E_w(X)/16$.

If to an edge an image belongs as in Fig.6.2 then the masking effect becomes too high. In blocks D1, D2, D3 and D4 in comparison of entire block proportionally to the local variances V the masking effect for a block D need to be reduced.

$$E_m(D) = \frac{E_w(D)\delta(D)}{16} \qquad (6.6)$$

Where $\delta(D) = (V(D1) + V(D2) + V(D3) + V(D4))/4V(D)$,

In block pixel values for the variance is given by V(D).

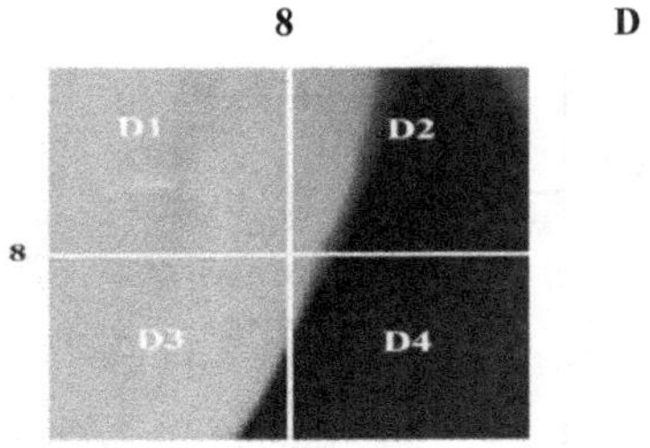

Fig 6.2: Block of an image contains an edge

Where C_{ij} is obtained from quantized JPEG table [10] on basis of CSF as shown in table 6.2.

Table 6.2: Values of C_{ij}

i\j	0	1	2	3	4	5	6	7
0	0	0.8264	1.0000	0.3906	0.1736	0.0625	0.0384	0.0269
1	0.6944	0.6944	0.5102	0.2770	0.1479	0.0297	0.0278	0.0331
2	0.5102	0.5917	0.3906	0.1736	0.0625	0.0308	0.0210	0.0319
3	0.5102	0.3460	0.2066	0.1189	0.0384	0.0132	0.0156	0.0260
4	0.308	0.206	0.073	0.031	0.021	0.008	0.009	0.016

	6	6	0	9	6	4	4	9
5	0.1736	0.0816	0.0331	0.0244	0.0152	0.0092	0.0078	0.0118
6	0.0416	0.0244	0.0164	0.0132	0.0094	0.0068	0.0069	0.0098
7	0.0193	0.0118	0.0111	0.0104	0.0080	0.0100	0.0094	0.0102

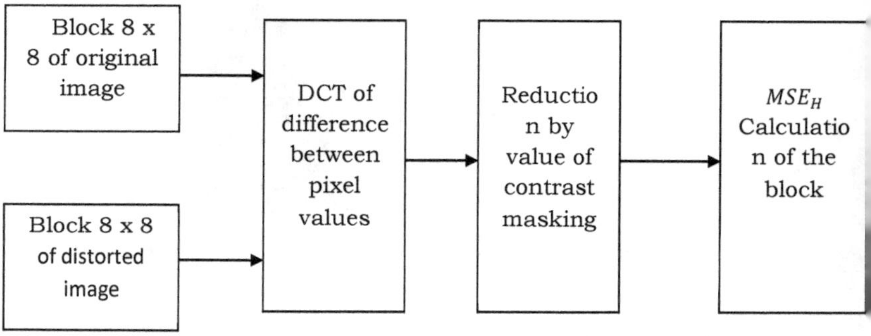

Fig 6.3: Flow-chart of PSNR_HVS_M calculation

The MSE_H is the MSE taken into account CSF i.e. reducing the value by contrast masking. Now, the maximal masking effect

$$E_{max} = \max\left(E_m\,(X_e), E_m(X_d)\right) \quad (6.7)$$

The distorted image block's of DCT coefficients, original image blocks are represented by X_e and X_d. In the following manner then X_e and X_d difference is determined as

$$X_{\Delta ij} = \begin{cases} X_{eij} - X_{dij}, & i = 0, j = 0 \\ 0, & \left|X_{eij} - X_{dij}\right| \le E_{norm}/C_{ij} \\ X_{eij} - X_{dij} - E_{norm}/C_{ij}, & X_{eij} - X_{dij} > E_{norm}/C_{ij} \end{cases} \quad (6.8)$$

$$X_{eij} - X_{dij} + E_{norm}/C_{ij}\text{, otherwise}$$

Where $E_{norm} = \sqrt{E_{max}/64}$.

6.2.4 Structural Similarity (SSIM) Index

In an image on the basis of measurement of structural information a new philosophy is proposed for image QA, and in the research area it has gained significant visibility. Between a distorted image, reference image there is an occurrence of visibility errors and these visibility errors (differences) are quantified and the reason for these errors are the properties of human visual system

The very composite and non linear system is HVS, but on linear operators maximum number of the previous models is based and with the help of restricted and simplistic stimuli these have been characterised. On a number of generalizations and strong assumptions the error-sensitivity approaches are depended. A brief summary is given below.

The Quality Definition Problem

The image quality definition is the most fundamental problem. In particular, it is not clear that with loss of quality the error visibility should be equated. By a global scale factor the multiplication of the image intensities is an obvious example. Between image quality and image fidelity the correlation is moderate and it is suggested by several studies.

The Suprathreshold Problem

Under much error sensitivity models the psychophysical experiments lie and these are specifically designed so that, the threshold can be estimated. The visual error sensitivity measures are defined by using CSF and various masking effects which are the measured threshold values. However, such near-threshold models can be generalized or not indicated by very few psychophysical studies. For analyzing image distortions the suprathreshold psychophysics have been incorporated.

Natural Image Complexity Problem

The spots, bars, or sinusoidal gratings are relatively simple patterns and using these most of the psychophysical experiments are conducted. For example, from threshold experiments the CSF is typically obtained with the help of global sinusoidal images. Using a superposition of two (or perhaps a few) the masking phenomena are usually characterized. But than the real world images all such patterns are much simpler. Recently both simple and complex patterns are included in established Modelfest dataset[40], and should facilitate future studies.

De-correlation Problem

For spatially pooling errors when a Minkowski metric is chosen to use and at different locations the errors are statistically independent which is assumed indirectly. This case is true if the input signals to the pooling eliminated dependencies is prior to the processing.

However, for linear channel decomposition methods this case is not appropriate and the example of the linear channel decomposition is wavelet transform. In wavelet coefficients of natural images i.e., between intra- and inter-channel a strong dependency exists and in [6] it has been shown. In fact, by spoiling this strong dependency by the wavelet image compression techniques the success is achieved. For the purpose of interaction between coefficients we use various visual masking models. Statistically, the control model is gained by a well-designed nonlinear gain it has been shown, in which to reduce dependencies the parameters are optimized rather than fitting the data from masking experiments, and there is a great reduction in dependencies of the transform coefficients. The statistical, perceptual dependencies are reduced with the help of optimal design of transformation and masking models. We have to see what extend there is an improvement in current quality assessment algorithms performance and this is shown by these models.

Cognitive Interaction Problem

The perceived quality of images is influenced by cognitive understanding (e.g., eye movements). For example, with different instructions if s/he is provided [11] then to the same image different quality scores are given by a human observer. The image quality [11] evaluation may be effected by the earlier information which regards the image content. But these effects are not considered by most image quality metrics, as they are difficult to understand and quantify.

The image degradations is considered by this philosophy because in structural information variation there are recognized changes. The top-down approach is a new paradigm. The suprathreshold problem is avoided by it because to quantify the perceived distortions on threshold psychophysics it does not rely. On the other hand, to a certain extent there is a reduction in cognitive interaction problem and the reason for reduction is that when object structures are probed, it is observed that the process is for visual observation, which includes the high level and interactive processes. To some extent there is a elimination of natural image complexity and de-correlation problems.

To evaluate the structural changes between two signals having complex structure signals a new philosophy is proposed. Hence, the reason why SSIM is modelled is that it is assumed that the human visual perception is highly adapted for the extraction of the structural information.

The SSIM metric [17] is proposed by Zhou Wang et. al.,. They indicated as the product of the illumination, reflectance the luminance of an object surface is observed, but in the scene the object structure is illumination independent. Consequently, in an image the illumination is a separated to explore the structural information. For an image by it's structural information the object structure is represented and it is independent of contrast and average luminance. Since across a scene there is a variation in luminance and contrast.

The luminance, contrast & structure comparison are three tasks corresponds for subjective evaluation implicitly in the SSIM index. The image patches are carried out locally by using these comparisons. First, for each signal the comparison of luminance is done. As the mean intensity (μ) this is estimated assuming discrete signals

$$\mu_x = \frac{1}{N}\sum_{i=1}^{N} x_i \tag{6.9}$$

Second, from the signal the mean intensity is removed. An estimate of the signal contrast is the standard deviation.

$$\sigma_x = \left(\frac{1}{N-1}\sum_{i=1}^{N}(x_i - \mu_x)^2\right) \tag{6.10}$$

Thirdly, with its own standard deviation the signal is normalized, so that the two signals having unit standard deviation are compared. Finally, to provide an overall similarity measure the three components are combined:

$$S(x,y) = f(l(x,y), c(x,y), s(x,y)) \tag{6.11}$$

The following properties are satisfied by SSIM.

- Symmetry: $S(x,y) = S(y,x)$ When among two signals the resemblance is enumerated, it should not concern the result while interchanging the input signal order.
- Boundedness: $S(x,y) \leq 1$. How close the two signals are to being completely the same is provided as the warning.
- Unique maximum: $S(x,y) = 1$ iff x=y. the count of any variations between input signals measured by SSIM.

The structure comparison, contrast comparison & luminance comparison are the comparison functions

$$l(x,y) = \frac{2\mu_x\mu_y + C_1}{\mu_x^2 + \mu_y^2 + C_1} \quad (6.12)$$

$$c(x,y) = \frac{2\sigma_x\sigma_y + C_2}{\sigma_x^2 + \sigma_y^2 + C_2} \quad (6.13)$$

$$s(x,y) = \frac{\sigma_{xy} + C_3}{\sigma_x\sigma_y + C_3} \quad (6.14)$$

Here $C_1 = (K_1 L)^2$ and $K_1 \ll 1$, $C_2 = (K_2 L)^2$ and $K_2 \ll 1$, $C_3 = C_2/2$ and L represents the range of pixel values in dynamic.

Therefore this results in below equation:

$$SSIM(x,y) = \frac{(2\mu_x\mu_y)(2\sigma_{xy})}{(\mu_x^2 + \mu_y^2 + C_1)(\sigma_x^2 + \sigma_y^2 + C_2)} \quad (6.15)$$

Here the mean of X & Y signals are μ_x, μ_y and σ_x, σ_y is variance of X & Y signals

$$\mu_x = \sum_{i=1}^{N} w_i x_i \quad (6.16)$$

$$\sigma_x = \left(\sum_{i=1}^{N} w_i (x_i - \mu_x)^2\right) \quad (6.17)$$

$$\sigma_{xy} = \sum_{i=1}^{N} w_i (x_i - \mu_x)(y_i - \mu_y) \quad (6.18)$$

Where for 11×11 (w) the circular-symmetric Gaussian weighs function is given by w_i

$w = \{w_i | i = 1,2,\ldots,N\}$.

$C_1 = C_2 = 0$, which generate unstable results while both $(\mu_x^2 + \mu_y^2)$ or $(\sigma_x^2 + \sigma_y^2)$ is very nearer to zero.

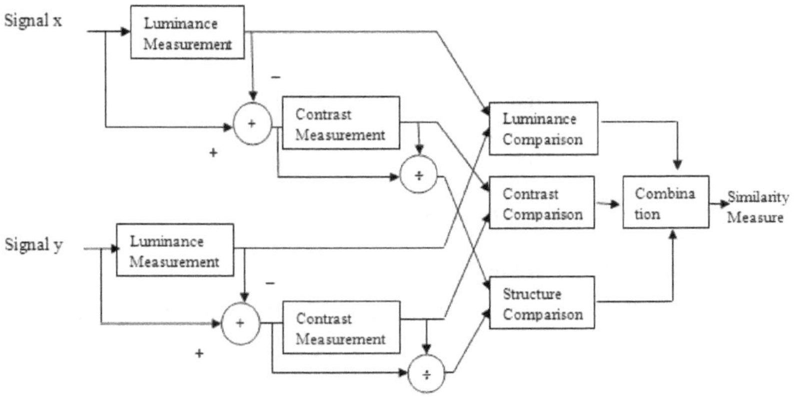

Fig 6.4: SSIM measurement systems

In general using index Mean SSIM (MSSIM) the overall image quality can be evaluated

$$MSSIM(X,Y) = \frac{1}{M} SSIM(x_j, y_j) \tag{6.19}$$

Here the reference and distorted images are denoted by X & Y, at the jth local window the images data is denoted by x_j & y_j; and the No. of local windows of the image is represented by M.

6.2.5 Normalized Cross Correlation (NK)

In seismology, for the purpose of searching signals which are repetitive in a time series and the entire process is known as matched filtering and here we use correlation frequently. Since the huge numbers are obtained by the correlation of two huge amplitude signals, when the amplitude of the cross correlation are compared then only one can confirm the similarity of two signals.

Normalized Cross-Correlation checks the similarity between the reference data and extracted data.

$$NK = \frac{\sum_{x,y} N_{x,y} \bar{N}_{x,y}}{\sum_{x,y} (N_{x,y})^2} \quad (6.20)$$

as reference image pixel N is defined and as extracted image pixel $\bar{N}$ is defined. Here NK$\in$ [0, 1] and NK=0 means N and $\bar{N}$ are completely uncorrelated, NK=1 means N and $\bar{N}$ are highly correlated [17].

6.2.6 Bit Error Rate (BER)

The Bit Error Rate [1] is the resemblance between the reference image and extracted image.

$$BER = \frac{INCORRECT}{TOTAL} \quad (6.21)$$

Whereas as the No. of incorrect bits in the extracted image the INCORRECT is considered, and in the Input image & BER $\in$ [0, 1] as the total No. of bits *the* TOTAL is considered.

6.2.7 Embedding Capacity

As a resultant image or watermarked image the embedded capacity is the total number of bits that can be embedded. To know the performance of embedding method this measurement metric is used. In the near reversible scheme we imply that NK ought to be closer to the most extreme 1 and BER ought to be closer to the greatest 0. The lower limits of NK & BER cannot be settled for a near reversible but it can be settled for an application as wanted.

6.3 S.GUJJUNOORI SCHEME

The S.Gujjunoori et.al., scheme taken input as reference image, it is partitioned in to 8 X 8 blocks of entire input image. On each block of 8 X 8 get their intensity values and 2D DCT is applied. Every block of 8 X 8 is divided by default quantization table. The data is embedded when non-zero coefficients of DCT is greater than zero then the embedding procedure begins it continues until each and every 8 X 8 block of DCT to complete this is also known as embedding process. To embed the data the log function is used. Because of greater difference between the original Non-zero coefficients of AC, embedded coefficient so many blocking artifacts have been obtained in the watermarked image. The embedding capacity, robustness and visual quality is partially achieved by this scheme, but many blocking artifacts can be observed in the embedded image [75].

6.4 NRDH_MATH SCHEME

In NRDH_MATH scheme, the embedding process concentrates on achieving the better visual quality and removing the blocking artifacts. We propose a mathematical function to achieve the above objective. In each and every block of nonzero AC coefficients embed the data except the blocks which are nearer to zero or equal to zero. By reducing the modification to the coefficients of original the better visual quality in the proposed scheme. The coefficients of watermark are retained back the values nearer to the coefficients of original.

6.4.1 HVS BASED DATA EMBEDDING PROCESS

In the embedding progression the image is considered as input. Input image is Partition in to the 8 X 8 blocks. Each 8X8 is processed by the DCT to get DCT coefficients. To get the coefficients of DCT quantized the quantization is applied on the DCT coefficients, and then the embedding process is performed.

To embed the data when the secret bit is 0 and 1 by using function 6.23 all the Coefficients of Non-zero Quantized DCT are considered. This process should be continued for the entire image of 8 X 8 blocks and all coefficients of Non-zero quantized DCT of image. Lastly combined all the embedded blocks of 8 X 8 to obtain the embedded image after embedding.

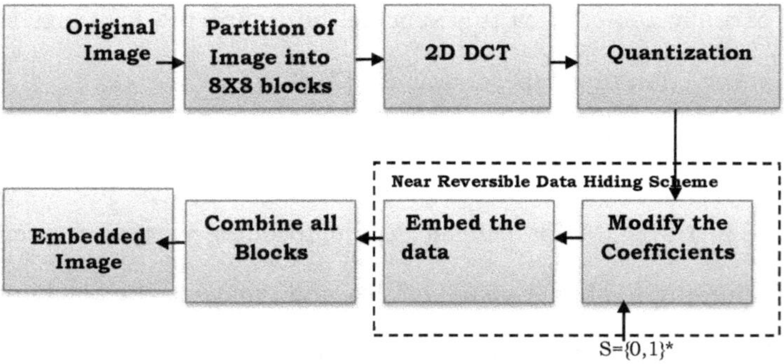

Fig 6.5: Embedding process of NRDH_MATH

6.4.2 HVS BASED DATA EMBEDDING ALGORITHM OF NRDH_MATH

Algorithm:

Step 1. Take an input image I and

Step 2. Partition I using DCT $I \rightarrow \{B_1, B_2, \ldots . B_l\}$

For each $B_j \in I$, where $1 \leq j \leq 8$

(a) Quantization of the DCT Coefficients in B_j .

for $i_1 \leftarrow 1$ to 8 do

for $i_2 \leftarrow 1$ to 8 do

$$C_j(i_1, i_2) = B_j(i_1, i_2)/Q(i_1, i_2);$$

end

end

(b) Compute T as shown in equation (6.22) after converting the matrix to row or column vectorization, If T > 0, then all the non-zero AC coefficients are modified and embed the data using equation (6.23). Let the resultant block be C_j.

Step 3. Into I= $\{C_{1,}C_2, \ldots . C_l\}$ all the C_j blocks are combined.

Step 4. For all the blocks repeat step 1 to step 3.

$$T = \sum_{j=2}^{64} c_j \qquad (6.22)$$

$$e = \begin{cases} \frac{c}{|c|}\left|\sqrt[0.94]{c} * 0.9\right| & \text{if } S = 0, \\ \frac{c}{|c|}\left|\left(\sqrt[1.2]{c} * 1.5\right) - 1\right| & \text{if } S = 1. \end{cases} \qquad (6.23)$$

Where c is the original Non-zero AC coefficient, S be the secret bit and e will be resultant version of c. Here |c| is round of c.

6.4.3 HVS BASED DATA EXTRACTION PROCESS OF NRDH_MATH

The Data embedding procedure is different from the Data extraction procedure. Extraction process considers an embedded image as input. The embedding image is partitioned in to 8X8 blocks. From the modified structure the data bits are extracted and restore in which all the Non-zero quantized DCT Coefficients of embedded image from the equation 6.24 and 6.25. The dequantization and IDCT will be applied on each 8X8 blocks of image. Finally all the original coefficients of the image 8X8 blocks are combined so that the original image is obtained.

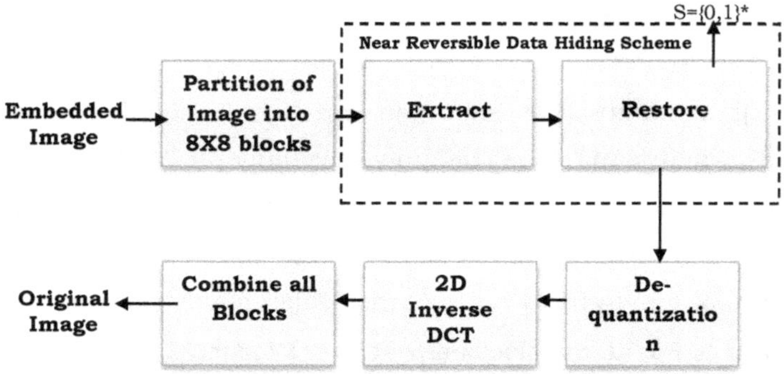

Fig 6.6: Extraction Process of NRDH_MATH

6.4.4 HVS BASED DATA EXTRACTION ALGORITHM OF NRDH_MATH

Algorithm:

Step 1. Take a watermarked input image (I)

Step 2. Extract C_j from $I \leftarrow \{C_1, C_2, \ldots C_l\}$.

Step 3. For each $C_j \in I$

When $T > 0$

Extraction of data bits using (6.24).

Restore of modified coefficients using (6.25).

The resultant block to be E_j.

Step 4. Dequantize of elements E_j as:

for $i_1 \leftarrow 1$ to 8 do

for $i_2 \leftarrow 1$ to 8 do

$R_j(i_1, i_2) = E_j(i_1, i_2) \times Q(i_1, i_2);$

End

End

Step 5. All the blocks to combine R_j to obtain I i.e. $I = \{R_1, R_2, \ldots, R_l\}$

Step 6. For all embedded $R_j \in I$, repeat step 1 to step 5.

$$I_j = \begin{cases} 0 & \text{if } e\%2 = 0, \\ 1 & \text{otherwise.} \end{cases} \quad (6.24)$$

$$\bar{c} = \begin{cases} \frac{e}{|e|} |(e/0.9)^{0.94}| \\ \frac{e}{|e|} |(e/1.5)^{1.2} - 1| \end{cases} \quad (6.25)$$

Where for original c the restored version is $\bar{c}$. Here |e| refer to round of e.

Note that the data embedding, data extraction is Near Reversible.

6.5 RESULT AND ANALYSIS

We have implemented our proposed scheme using MATLAB. We used 512 × 512 GIF formatted grayscale images in the implementation.

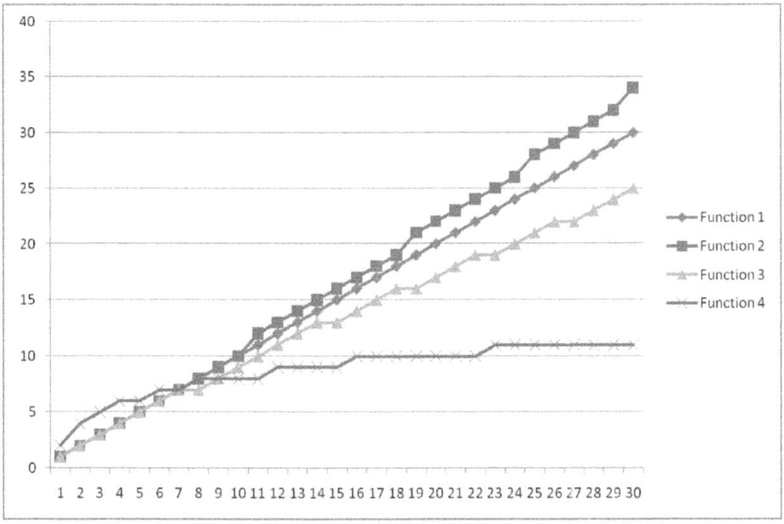

Fig 6.7: Behaviour of S.Gujjunoori et.al., function and NRDH_MATH functions

The proposed scheme with well suitable equation and also to evaluate HVS quality metrics like PSNR_HVS_M, PSNR_HVS, PSNR,

and MSSIM. Finally the Near Reversible Data Hiding Scheme provides higher quality metric values.

Where Function 1 is y=AC coefficients of original image,

Function 2 is $y = \left|\sqrt[0.94]{c} * 0.9\right|$

Function 3 is $y = \left|\left(\sqrt[1.2]{c} * 1.5\right) - 1\right|$

And Function 4 is $y = \lfloor 2\log_2(2|c|) \rfloor$

Where c represents the non-zero AC coefficient and y will be the modified value of c.

From the figure 6.7 & table 6.3, we can observe that the function 4 changes drastically with respect to their original coefficients which cause the distortion or blocking artifacts. From function 2 and function 3 graphs it is observed that the pixel values are nearer to function 1.

Table 6.3: Behaviour of S.Gujjunoori et.al., function and NRDH_MATH functions

S.No	Non-zero Quantized DCT Coefficients	(S.Gujjunoori et.al.,) Function-4	(NRDH_MATH) Function-2	(NRDH_MATH) Function-3
1	1	2	1	1
2	2	4	2	2
3	3	5	3	3
4	4	6	4	4
5	5	6	5	5
6	6	7	6	6
7	7	7	7	7
8	8	8	8	7
9	9	8	9	8
10	10	8	10	9
11	11	8	12	10
12	12	9	13	11
13	13	9	14	12
14	14	9	15	13
15	15	9	16	13
16	16	10	17	14
17	17	10	18	15
18	18	10	19	16
19	19	10	21	16
20	20	10	22	17

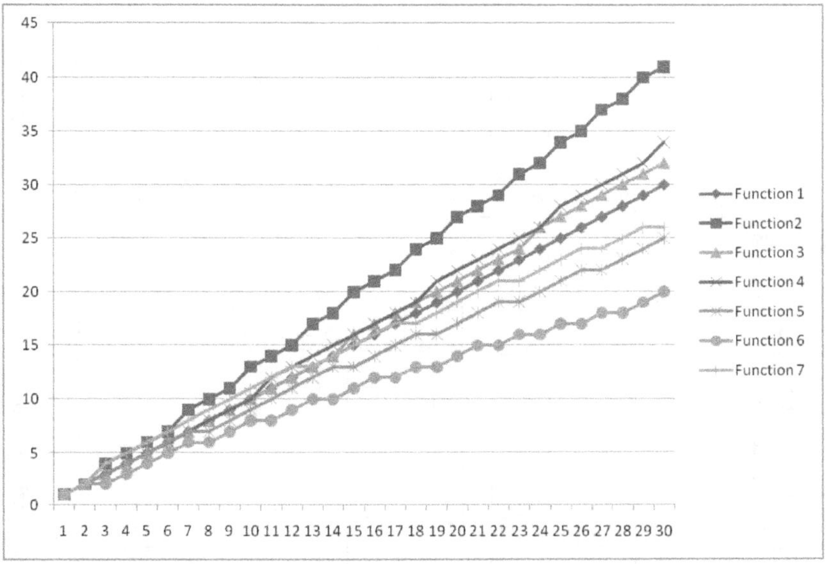

Fig 6.8: Behavior of various functions nearer to the NRDH_MATH function

Where Function 1 is y = AC coefficients of original image

Function 2 is $y = \left|\sqrt[0.94]{c} * 1.1\right|$

Function 3 is $y = \left|\sqrt[0.95]{c} * 0.9\right|$

Function 4 is $y = \left|\sqrt[0.94]{c} * 0.9\right|$

Function 5 is $y = \left|\left(\sqrt[1.2]{c} * 1.5\right) - 1\right|$

Function 6 is $y = \left|\left(\sqrt[1.2]{c} * 1.5\right) - 1\right|$

Function 7 is $y = \left|\left(\sqrt[1.3]{c} * 2\right) - 1\right|$

Table 6.4: Behavior of various functions nearer to the NRDH_MATH functions

	Actual Coefficients	Behavior of various functions nearer to the NRDH_MATH functions					
		Function-2	Function-3	NRDH_MATH Function-4	NRDH_MATH Function-5	Function-6	Function-7
	1	1	1	1	1	1	1
	2	2	2	2	2	2	2
	3	4	3	3	3	2	4
	4	5	4	4	4	3	5
	5	6	5	5	5	4	6
	6	7	6	6	6	5	7
	7	9	7	7	7	6	8
	8	10	8	8	7	6	9
	9	11	9	9	8	7	10
	10	13	10	10	9	8	11
	11	14	11	12	10	8	12
	12	15	12	13	11	9	13
	13	17	13	14	12	10	13
	14	18	14	15	13	10	14
	15	20	16	16	13	11	15
	16	21	17	17	14	12	16
	17	22	18	18	15	12	17
	18	24	19	19	16	13	17
	19	25	20	21	16	13	18
	20	27	21	22	17	14	19

Where c be the original non-zero AC coefficient and y be the resultant value of c. Here among six functions we can observe two functions nearer to function 1 than other functions are function 4 and function 5. Hence the above two quations are considered in code because they retain maximum values to original values. Here we have chosen function 4 and 5 for hiding the data from figure 6.8 & table 6.4.

Table 6.5: Embedded Capacity of S.Gujjunoori et.al., and NRDH_MATH scheme values

Images	Embedded Capacity	
	S.Gujjunoori et.al., Scheme	NRDH_MATH Scheme
aerial	56562	56562
airplane	12608	12608
baboon	74002	74002
barb	39346	39346
boat	36279	36279
couple	34360	34360
elaine	27556	27556
goldhill	38190	38190
lena	30767	30767
pentagon	50125	50125
pepper	33618	33618
truck	36734	36734
Zelda	20071	20071

Fig 6.9: Comparison of Capacity

The S.Gujjunoori et.al., scheme (in blue color) and NRDH_MATH scheme (in red color) address same which is observed from the table 6.5 & figure 6.9. And for some images there are more number of non-zero AC coefficients, we achieve higher capacity and whenever there is less number of non-zero AC coefficients, we achieve equal capacity.

Table 6.6: Normal corelation of S.Gujjunoori et.al., & NRDH_MATH scheme values

Images	Normal correlation	
	S.Gujjunoori et. al., Scheme	NRDH_MATH Scheme
aerial	0.998	1.0002
airplane	0.9997	1.0001
baboon	0.9979	1.0001
barb	0.9982	1.0001
boat	0.9983	1.0003
couple	0.9977	1
elaine	0.9991	1.0001
goldhill	0.9988	1.0001
lena	0.9975	1.0004
pentagon	0.9989	1.0001

pepper	0.9979	1.0002
truck	0.9991	1.0001
Zelda	0.9992	1.0001

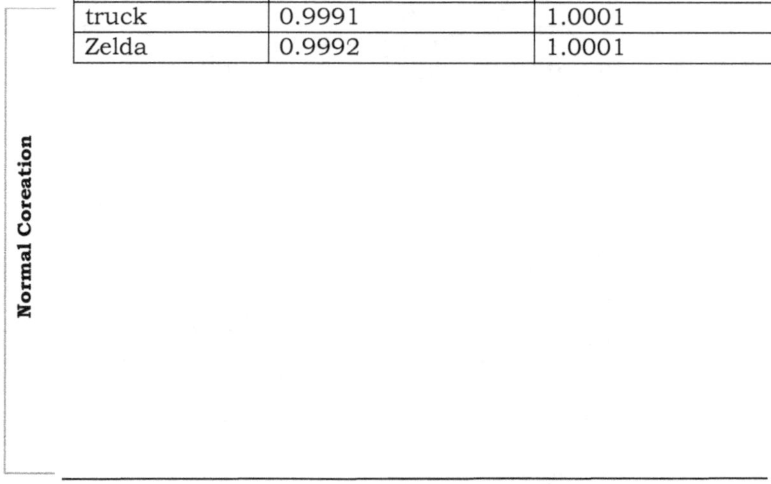

Fig 6.10: Comparison of NK

As the Normalized Cross-Correlation checks the similarity between images where NK ∈ [0, 1] and more the value near to one the more they are highly correlated, we can achieve them from table 6.6 & figure 6.10 that the NRDH_MATH scheme (in red color) achieve values more nearer to one than the S.Gujjunoori et.al., scheme (in blue color). Hence, NRDH_MATH scheme is highly correlated and NRDH_MATH scheme achieves better NK than the S.Gujjunoori et.al., scheme.

Table 6.7: PSNR of S.Gujjunoori et.al., and NRDH_MATH scheme values

Images	PSNR	
	S.Gujjunoori et.al., Scheme	**NRDH_MATH Scheme**
aerial	32.141	61.7422
airplane	40.7976	69.834
baboon	33.469	66.6945
barb	34.9173	66.7124
boat	34.9788	63.9764
couple	35.0741	60.1201
elaine	37.8969	66.3174

goldhill	37.2432	67.5262
lena	35.2476	63.1417
pentagon	36.7206	69.0365
pepper	35.5128	63.5586
truck	39.6642	73.0579
zelda	40.2902	72.2345

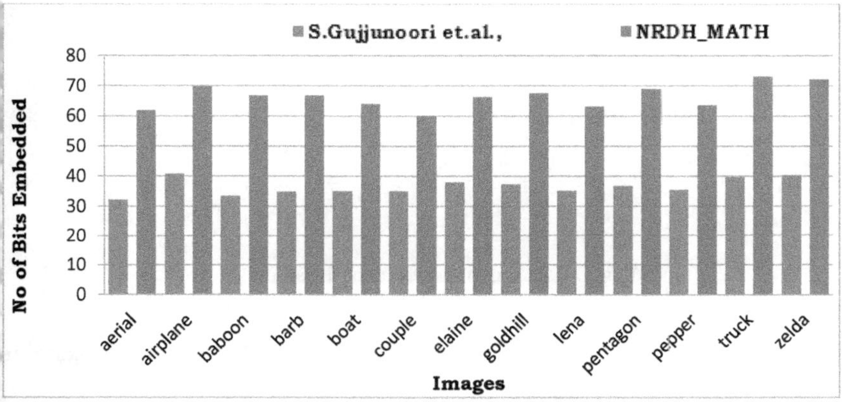

Fig 6.11: Comparison of PSNR

In figure table 6.7 & 6.11 it is observed that the NRDH_MATH scheme represents in red color, better results achieved for PSNR, besides the S.Gujjunoori et.al., scheme represents in blue color.

Table 6.8: MSSIM of S.Gujjunoori et.al., and NRDH_MATH scheme values

Images	MSSIM	
	S.Gujjunoori et.al., Scheme	NRDH_MATH Scheme
aerial	0.977	0.9952
airplane	0.995	0.9985
baboon	0.9809	0.9976
barb	0.983	0.9969
boat	0.9824	0.9958
couple	0.983	0.9969
elaine	0.9871	0.9971

goldhill	0.9837	0.9972
lena	0.9836	0.9952
pentagon	0.9813	0.9978
pepper	0.9849	0.9951
truck	0.9863	0.9988
Zelda	0.9888	0.9989

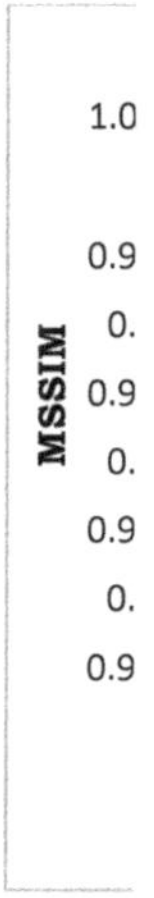

Fig 6.12: Comparison of MSSIM

We can observe from table 6.8 & figure 6.12 that the NRDH_MATH scheme (in red color) achieves better results for MSSIM i.e. results are nearer to one (structures in embedded image are more similar to Original image). Therefore, than the S.Gujjunoori et.al., scheme (in blue color) the better result for MSSIM is achieved by NRDH_MATH scheme.

Table 6.9: PSNR_HVS of S.Gujjunoori et.al., and NRDH_MATH scheme values

Images	PSNR_HVS	
	S.Gujjunoori et.al., Scheme	**NRDH_MATH Scheme**
aerial	25.8168	30.5758
airplane	34.1044	37.3014
baboon	27.9046	35.1301
barb	29.4258	35.1043
boat	28.3857	32.1248
couple	29.1022	34.0478
elaine	30.9839	35.1421
goldhill	30.537	35.4885
lena	28.386	31.7454
pentagon	30.1236	37.3714
pepper	28.8172	32.333

truck	33.2026	41.0897
Zelda	33.3486	40.5373

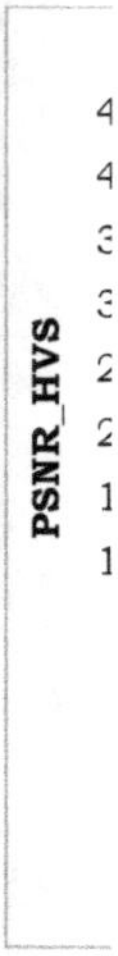

Fig 6.13: Comparison of PSNR_HVS

We can observe from table 6.9 & figure 6.13 that the NRDH_MATH scheme (in red color) achieves better results for all the images than the S.Gujjunoori et.al., scheme (in blue color) for PSNR_HVS. Therefore, NRDH_MATH Scheme outperforms the S.Gujjunoori et.al., scheme.

Table 6.10: PSNR_HVS_M of S.Gujjunoori et.al., and NRDH_MATH scheme values

Images	PSNR_HVS_M	
	S.Gujjunoori et.al., Scheme	**NRDH_MATH Scheme**
aerial	27.7434	32.0989
airplane	35.7368	38.5642
baboon	30.5262	37.2993
barb	30.9697	36.2757
boat	29.9767	33.3077
couple	31.102	35.989
elaine	32.1784	36.2087
goldhill	31.9684	36.5304
lena	29.8235	32.839
pentagon	31.8058	38.779
pepper	30.2371	33.4329
truck	34.7113	42.2659

Zelda	34.5154	41.845

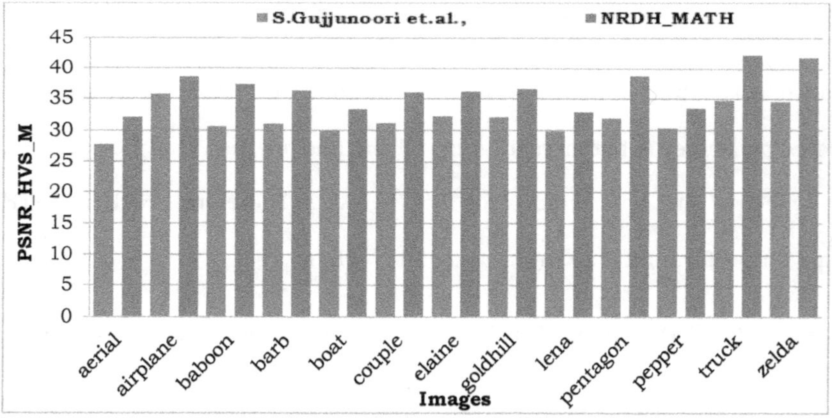

Fig 6.14: Comparison of PSNR_HVS_M

We can observe from table 6.10 & figure 6.14 that the NRDH_MATH scheme (in red color) achieves better results for PSNR_HVS_M for all the images than the S.Gujjunoori et.al., scheme (in blue color). The NRDH_MATH scheme achieves better results than S.Gujjunoori et.al., scheme

Table 6.11: BER of S.Gujjunoori et.al., and RDH_MATH scheme values

Images	BER	
	S.Gujjunoori et.al., Scheme	**NRDH_MATH Scheme**
aerial	27.7434	32.0989

airplane	35.7368	38.5642
baboon	30.5262	37.2993
barb	30.9697	36.2757
boat	29.9767	33.3077
couple	31.102	35.989
elaine	32.1784	36.2087
goldhill	31.9684	36.5304
lena	29.8235	32.839
pentagon	31.8058	38.779
pepper	30.2371	33.4329
truck	34.7113	42.2659
Zelda	34.5154	41.845

Fig 6.15: Comparison of Bit Error Rate

We can observe from table 6.11 & figure 6.15 that the S.Gujjunoori scheme (in blue color) achieves result for bit error rate is nearer to 0.1 i.e. nearer to zero where as NRDH_MATH scheme (in red color) achieves values for bit error rate is in range of 0.4 to 0.5. Therefore, when compared to the bit error rate of NRDH_MATH scheme the S.Gujjunoori scheme performance is better.

We present different images from figure 6.16-6.22(Barb, boat, couple, Elaine, Lena, Pepper and Zelda) of GIF format of size 512×512 in the following and their corresponding distorted images can also be observed from all the observations, we can find that the S.Gujjunoori et.al., scheme distorted images more where as the NRDH_MATH scheme achieves better visual quality.

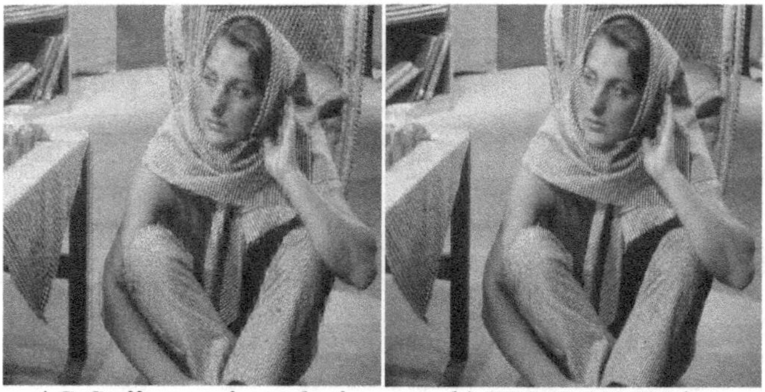

a) S.Gujjunoori et.al., image b) NRDH_MATH image

Fig 6.16: Embedded Barb image of S.Gujjunoori et.al., and NRDH_MATH scheme

a) S.Gujjunoori et.al., image b) NRDH_MATH watermark image

Fig 6.17: Embedded Boat image of S.Gujjunoori et.al., and NRDH_MATH scheme

a) S.Gujjunoori et.al., image b) NRDH_MATH image

Fig 6.18: Embedded Couple image of S.Gujjunoori et.al., and NRDH_MATH scheme

a) S.Gujjunoori et.al., image b) NRDH_MATH image
Fig 6.19: Embedded Elaine image of S.Gujjunoori et.al., and NRDH_MATH scheme

a) S.Gujjunoori et.al., image b) NRDH_MATH image
Fig 6.20: Embedded Lena image of S.Gujjunoori et.al., and NRDH_MATH scheme

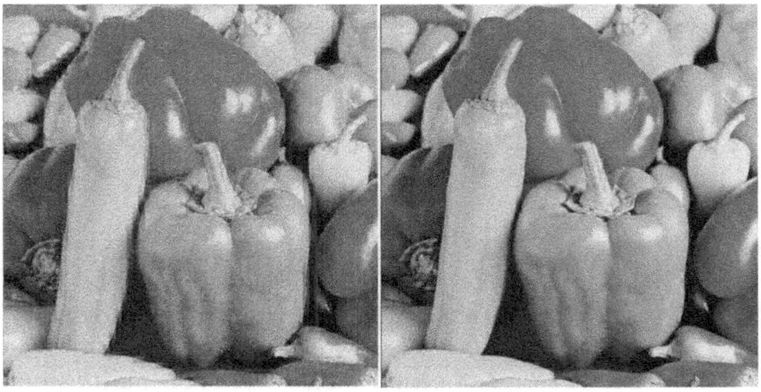

a) S.Gujjunoori et.al., image b) NRDH_MATH image:
Fig 6.21: Embedded Pepper image of S.Gujjunoori et.al., and NRDH_MATH scheme

a) S.Gujjunoori et.al., image b)NRDH_MATH image
Fig 6.22: Embedded Zelda image of S.Gujjunoori et.al., and NRDH_MATH scheme

6.6 SUMMARY

In the category of NRDH there is a requirement of more sophisticated scheme. The near reversible schemes are to be addressed in many applications of remote sensing. Many blocking artifacts creates by the S.Gujjunoori et.al., scheme due to use of log function it results, degrades the visual quality and the coefficients with greater difference is transformed by it. The visual quality in high amount is achieved in the NRDH_MATH scheme by using the suitable equation and for the Embedded Coefficients there is a minimization of difference between the Original Non-zero AC Coefficients.

6.7 DATASET DESCRIPTION

The collection of digitized images in a image database of USC-SIPI. It is maintained primarily so that the research can be maintained in machine vision, image processing and image analysis. In 1977 the distribution of

USC-SIPI image database first edition was completed and since then there is addition of many new images.

The volumes of database is divided into 256x256 pixels, 512x512 pixels, or 1024x1024 pixels are the images of different sizes. For black and white images all images are 8 bits/pixel and for color images 24 bits/pixel.

Chapter - 7

CONCLUSION & FUTURE WORK

7.1 CONCLUSION

The Reversibility and Near Reversibility is demanding for the applications like military communications, remote sensing, etc. the wide usage and the close association of DCT with the digital contents. The need for the data embedding schemes which working DCT by achieving the reversibility and near reversibility. Balancing the limitations existed among the embedding capacity, visual quality and the reversibility and near reversibility requirement is challenging. Further, while embedding the data to achieve higher visual quality using the HVS characteristics, the metric used to evaluate the distorted content should have incorporated the same HVS characteristic considered. In this thesis achieved embedding capacity and visual quality using several data embedding schemes are proposed. All the schemes are towards achieving the reversibility and near reversibility using the DCT. The HVS based metrics of visual quality are like PSNR_HVS, PSNR_HVS_M etc., metrics are proposed

for evaluation of the embedded digital content using the HVS characteristics.

7.2 FUTURE WORK

In this thesis, all proposed data hiding techniques embed data into QCIF formatted videos and grey scale images in frequency domain. The data embedding into color image and videos are also possible. The majority of the proposed data embedding schemes embed the data into the I- frames during the MPEG-4 compression. The data embedding into P-frame and B- frames of the MPEG-4 is also possible.